# *Single One*

## Pastor Lydia E. Torres

SINGLE ONE

Copyright © 2020 by Lydia E. Torres

Single One

Published in the United States of America
ISBN 978-1-7340305-6-3

All rights are reserved solely by the author. The author declares that the contents are original and do not infringe on the rights of any other person.

No part of this book may be reproduced in any form except with permission from the author.

All scripture references and quotations are taken from the Holy Bible, KJV, used by permission.

*SINGLE ONE*

## Dedication

This book is dedicated to my daughter Shalayia a beautiful young woman who I love very much and to all the single women who are trying to understand themselves and to understand how to navigate through life in the face of a changing world. This book is also dedicated to single men who are trying to figure out how to live single with the eventual desire to marry one day.

I was once a single woman who married a little later than all my friends but do not regret it at all. I too had many unanswered questions about relationship, love, men, family and building an independent life outside of my immediate family. This book is just a springboard into a discussion of many types of problems single woman and men face on a daily basis. Navigating through all these issues can leave a young woman or man feeling overwhelmed and frustrated. The dating scene alone has changed so much that it has become unrecognizable.

## SINGLE ONE

## Forward

Dating rituals have changed and the focus has become more about women having to please a man just so they get a call back, commitment and or marriage. The other case is one where a woman lacks total respect for a man and basically uses him to obtain monetary compensation, an apartment, car or other luxuries they desire. Whatever happened to dating someone out of real love, care or concern for another human being? Whatever happened to courtship, respect and a man being a gentleman? Ladies men will treat you the way you allow them to treat you. Chasing a man shows the man how desperate you are. Men don't like desperate women. Desperate women make men draw back in the long run. Men love strong women that are not overpowering or obnoxious. Men appreciate a woman that is drama free as well.

A man respects a woman that has her life in order. For example, men love a woman who has a great handle over her own affairs. A woman who pays

## SINGLE ONE

her bills and isn't looking for a handout from a man. Men want to take care of women who don't need taking care of. Read that sentence again. Acting like a weak woman who needs a man's money is really a set up for the woman to become dependent on a man's finances. Though having a man that can take care of you is sweet, a woman should never expect or set up her life so a man is taking care of her. A relationship can come to a crashing end and if your finances are wrapped up in his pocket you will be left hanging dry when he walks away. Relationships are more than just a passing time and if that is what they are then do not release your financial independence to anyone.

I have grappled with all the topics discussed in this book and yet God has helped me get through each one with His love and my anger. In time my anger gave way to obedience and that one act changed the course of my life for the greater! The advice in this book is not intended to replace God's word or professional counseling but merely to help bring light to some of the concerns some singles may have. The advice comes from a woman that was single far longer than all her friends and who married a man God chose for her. Not out of desperation or because she had no other prospects but because God offered her a better plan than the one she was counting on for her life.

To understand relationships, you must first understand who created relationships and what are the true responsibilities every person has within a relationship. Why have relationships become so unbalanced? The reasons relationships are unbalanced are many women have not consulted God nor made Him a priority but have chosen to make life, itself their god. Placing God first in your life gives way for God's hand to show up in your life.

In this book I will attempt to give the reader some useful information that is biblically based as well as practical sound advice that can help all singles go from Single to One in God. God said it best in **Genesis 2:24** "For this reason shall a man leave his Father and his Mother, and be joined to his

## SINGLE ONE

wife; and they shall become one flesh." (Matthew 19:5, Mark 10:8, Ephesians 5:31) God's desire is to take your singleness and join you to the one God has designed just for you. When God brings two people together,

He does so with the plan to cause them both to succeed and grow in love, wisdom, hope, joy and peace. It is in that growth that God can bring about the greatest of miracles.

May this book bring clarity and help you to choose wisely when you decide to finally settle down.

*SINGLE ONE*

# Table of Contents

| Chapter | Page |
|---|---|
| Rebellion | 11 |
| What Do Boys and Girls Need? | 19 |
| What is Family | 29 |
| Not a Prophet Among Your Own Family? | 37 |
| Leave Your Family | 46 |
| Get Rid of Sin | 52 |
| Trust | 58 |
| Courtship/Dating | 63 |
| What Makes for a Good Relationship? | 69 |
| A Good Man Not a Perfect Man | 76 |
| A Good Woman Not a Perfect One | 82 |
| Building a Healthy Family Structure | 87 |
| Real Marriage Talk | 91 |

**SINGLE ONE**

If Two Would Agree……..…..…………..96

Real Love………………………………..106

Sex, Sex, Sex……………………………111

Treat Her Like a Lady…………………119

Treat Him Like a Man…………………126

Who Can You Trust?..............................131

Go to the Word…………………………135

Put Family in Their Proper Place………..139

Get Rid of Filth……………………............143

Sexual Discrimination……..……………..147

It's Time to Tell Your Secret…...………...152

Communication...………………...............160

Your Work is Not in Vain…....…………….164

What's My Worth?......................................167

Where Is Your Love?..................................173

Who are You Listening To?........................175

*SINGLE ONE*

**Why Can't I Move Forward from This?**................................................179

**What Are You Planting in Your Life?**................................................183

**What's the Difference Between a Boyfriend and a Husband?**........................187

**What Are Men Really Thinking?**................191

**Loose the Nasty Girl!**...................................193

**Do You Know What You Want?**................199

**Red Flags!**......................................................204

**The Last Word/A Good & Perfect Father**………………………………...209

**Conclusion**………………..……………214

## **Chapter 1**
## *Rebellion*

When thinking about rebellion, stubbornness or disobedience it all comes down to one thing, your resentment about being told what to do. Why do we get so worked up when someone tells us what to do? Whether it's "Please clean up your room", "Don't talk to that person if they put doubt in your heart." Humans push back when they feel they are being told what to do. That inner push back is called rebellion.

# SINGLE ONE

The word rebellion means revolt, uprising, insurgence, upheaval, mutiny, revolution, rising, agitation, and insurrection. When we rebel against any type of good sound advice we are revolting or turning our back on the advice and the person who is giving us said advice. When we reject good advice, we are creating an insurgence. We have become an enemy army attacking the advice we have received. This rebellion creates upheaval in our hearts and in our emotions. Why, because while we may know the advice is sound we are rejecting it not on its merits but rather just because we choose not to hear it. Rebellion is mutiny because we are abandoning good sense, great logic and wisdom to hold on to our notion of what is right for us or what we want.

What is Rebellion? What does rebellion really mean in our lives?

1) Rebellion is the attempt to overthrow the government and assume control

## SINGLE ONE

2) Defiance of authority. Why is rebellion the over throwing of government because we are overthrowing God's wisdom and government for our own. Our rebellion tells God we are the rulers of our own world and we have no need for Him or His rule. Our rebellion is complete defiance just as shattering as the defiance that man showed God in the garden when He told Adam and Eve "of the tree of good and evil you shall not eat!" Eve defied God and then led Adam to do the same. Their defiance towards God created a separation from God that could only be healed by Jesus's death. An innocent God had to die to correct the defiance one man and one woman. Therefore, God hates rebellion but embraces obedience.

The opposite of the word Rebellion is compliance. The word compliance means obedience and fulfillment. The synonyms of compliance are; acquiescence, agreement, submission, amenability, passivity and to fall in line. Compliance is a readiness to comply and to

## SINGLE ONE

conform. Rebellion keeps us from conforming to God's will and locks us into an attitude of recalcitrance. The one place we should be showing recalcitrance is in our un-wavering determination to serve and love God!

We assume that people who ask us to do something that somehow, it's about control. Well if the person loves us, is looking out for us, there is no jealousy or personal gain to be made then that person is just trying to help you.

We react with resistance towards people because we make it an issue of control when it's about us refusing to accept there is an area where we need change. Change requires redirection of behavior. Without redirection or change in our mind, heart or behavior we cannot be changed. God tells us in His word that we are to be "born again, not of just water but of Spirit." This idea of being born again is really the idea of being transformed as a result of us yielding to God's ability to change us and takes us out of rebellion into obedience.

## SINGLE ONE

How does a person go from rebellion to obedience?

1) For a person to go from rebellion to obedience, the person must admit to himself or herself that they are being governed by their own desires and not God's will.

2) The person must examine their life and review every time they made a decision based on fear, personal whim or just because someone told them to do the opposite action of the one they took.

3) The person must realize that their stubbornness is not independence but rebellion. You don't have to touch fire to know that it burns. You can feel the heat from the fire so touching it would be immature and childish. I know this example seems extreme, but I have seen people do just that. The minute someone tells them "that guy or girl is not for you: they immediately become defensive and

## SINGLE ONE

go out and entrench themselves even further in the bad relationship. However, those unions always fail.

4) A person must also examine the source of their rebellion. For example, did they have an overbearing mother or father. Did the person have a controlling parent or (s) that made them feel suffocating so as adults they perceive all advice to be a controlling maneuver. A person trapped in this cycle must come to terms with what is really happening. My mom was a great cook and she believed healthy children were plump in appearance, so she emphasized overeating and she served you way too much food. My mom was boss. She controlled everything in my life, and she made no apologies for it. I pushed back in the area of eating. So, the more she tried to get me to eat the less I wanted to eat. This was the one area where I could control my life. As a result

## SINGLE ONE

of this behavior I developed an eating disordered (dimorphic- seeing oneself as heavy when you are not) that lasted for ten years. At my lowest point I weighed 98 pounds and I was 27 years old. I could count every rib and vertebrae bone in my back. My hair was brittle, and my skin was completely dry beyond normal. Every time I looked in the mirror, I saw myself as needing to lose another 3-5 pounds. This rebellion towards my mom had taken its tow on my body. It was during this terrible time in my life that I finally realized how I was using food as a tool of rebellion against my mother. When God gave me this revelation I cried for days! I didn't want to live this way anymore. Rebellion can take you to very low moments in your life and can even bring you to the brink of death. If you have an eating disorder, whether it's under eating or overeating, examine the real source of that abnormal relationship with food.

## SINGLE ONE

> Ask yourself why do I reject good sound advice from people who love and care for me? Why do I not want people to show me their love by caring enough about me to not want me to go in the wrong direction for my life?
>
> 5) Until the necessary changes take place in a person's life and the rebellion in the heart is removed a person is in danger of repeating the same bad behaviors and poor decisions repeatedly.

For our life's to be a blessing to others, we must show forth the changes God has made in our life's. It's the changes in our behavior, character, attitude and emotions that testify to the world of the power of God to transform.

Don't fight your own changes or the people who are trying to help you obtain those changes.

SINGLE ONE

## Chapter 2
### *What do boys and girls need?*

The first real relationship that women and men are exposed to is that of their parents or parent. This initial relationship can give boys and girls valuable information about how women and men interact with each other. There are a few factors that go into the making of emotionally unable men and women.

A girl without a father or significant positive

## SINGLE ONE

male role model in her life will find it difficult to understand male needs or male shortcomings. A girl whose father with holds affection or attention can grow up to believe she is not worthy of love. She may grow up thinking she must be extra sweet, kind or bend over backwards to obtain the favor of a man. A young girl learns firsthand from a father how to value herself, how to be treated by a man and how to communicate with a man in general. Researchers have found that girls suffer just as much loss not having a father, as do boys without a father. Girls who do not have a positive father role model or who have had a negative role model will struggle with managing authority in their lives. They will be defiant towards authority and will resist any attempts to yield to a man in any way. They will also suffer from issues of infidelity with partners because they will have severe trust issues.

Boys raised without a father or strong male role model will grow up with a lack of personal responsibility and a lack for guidance as to how

## SINGLE ONE

to be a man. These same boys will grow up with a sense of having to be the leader in the home when they are not prepared to occupy that role. These boys will lack skills in leadership, follow through behavior and exhibit a lack of self-control. Some mothers get it in a son's head that they are the "man of the house" further pushing them into role they are not prepared to occupy. Some mothers become the all and all for their sons so that they guilt them every time they try to set up relationships with other women. The science points to clear facts that boys and girls both need positive healthy role models where they can learn how to be healthy adults as they mature.

Our culture has so embraced single mother households that women need to raise their girls and boys to be strong, as they will belong to different societal circles as they grow up. While girl children and boy children need love, discipline, consistency, boundaries, and an active parental presence they also need healthy male

## SINGLE ONE

and female role models.

## What are the responsibilities of mothers concerning their sons?

1) A mother's role is to raise a man not a boy. Mothers who pamper and spoil their sons will end up with sons who expect all women to cater to their needs only because they have not been taught to care about other's needs over their own. Boys who are spoiled by their mothers grow up believing that women are on the earth just to please them. They are raised to think that they are entitled to all things without earning what they are given. Children including boys are not born to be ungrateful but rather they are taught this through repeated examples of ungrateful behavior being rewarded. When my oldest son was about five years old, he started to ask for candy by the checkout line in the supermarket (we never let them eat candy until they were about eight and only on

## SINGLE ONE

special occasions). He began asking me for candy repeatedly. I told him no and if you ask me again, I will spank you in the car. The cashier told me that I was the first parent all day that said no to her child and stuck to it. I told her it's because parents are too concerned with what people will think about them if their child cries or acts up. I told her I am not afraid of my child crying or acting up I am also not afraid to punish or spank my child. My child never asked for candy at the checkout line again. Why? Because he saw that his annoying asking could not break me. A parent cannot be afraid to be the parent. Children don't need friends they need parents.

2) Boys need to be taught that education is the way out of poverty and being successful is cool. Boys need to understand that hard work is a major key to success in life. Boys need to clean up

## SINGLE ONE

their rooms do laundry and stick to a schedule every night. (Responsibility)

3) Boys need to learn how to run a household on their own.

4) Boys are concrete thinkers (they see and hear in black and white) they must be given clear consistent directions.

5) Boys need to move physically especially when they are younger to release all of the energy they have to burn off every day.

6) Boys need to be part of a team because it teaches cooperation.

7) Boys need to be sincerely praised when they succeed at something.

8) Boys need to learn how things work, like changing a tire, a light bulb, painting a wall and caring for a pet.

9) Boys need to know practical things like how to shave, tie a tie or bow tie

*SINGLE ONE*

10) Boys need to learn how to coordinate their clothes especially because more boys than girls are color blind

11) Boys need to learn how to cook, clean, and do laundry so that they never feel helpless or dependent on a woman.

12) Boys need to learn how to handle finances at an early age. Having a savings account teaches a boy how to save and how to postpone their desires for instant gratification.

**What are the responsibilities mothers should teach their daughters?**

1) Girls need to know it's okay to be smart and smarter than a man.

2) Girls need to learn how to cook, clean, organize and change a tire.

3) Girls need to be taught not to rely on their looks, sexuality, or feminine ways to get what they want. Girls need to be taught to love themselves instead of relying on others to love them.

## SINGLE ONE

4) Girls need to be taught to respect their bodies and that their bodies are not for sale. They are a treasure and they must secure themselves like treasure.

5) Girls need to be taught how to defend their opinions with facts not feelings.

6) Girls need to be taught that they are deserving of respect wherever they go by everyone. Girls need to know they do not have to put up with bad or bullying behavior!

7) Girls need to be taught that their talents should never be overlooked by anyone. Girls need to be taught that it's okay to be the boss without being angry. A woman who can control her emotions will never have her decisions questioned.

8) Girls need to know how to save and spend wisely. Having a savings account early on helps a girl learn the value of making and keeping a dollar for a rainy day. I learned

## SINGLE ONE

how to save and shop from my mom. She would often tell me "If you don't need to spend a dollar don't! Save the dollar until you have ten."

9) Girls need to learn how to budget and run a household.

10) Girls need to know they can achieve academic success, own a home and have a profession. They don't have to envy anyone else to have these things.

11) Girls need to learn how to protect themselves against predators.

12) Girls need to be taught that they do not need a man to complete them.

Reality dictates that for parents to produced well-balanced human beings they have to be thoughtful in how they raise their children. Children raised with love, discipline, boundaries, respect for others, respect for authority, healthy values and a good moral attitude will do much better in life and with life then those children

## SINGLE ONE

who are deprived of a good strong caring upbringing.

My mom lost her mother at five and was raised by her grandparents. They loved her but they did not spoil her instead they taught her to value herself, how to work hard, be obedient and care about others. She was not a perfect person, but she was able to raise hard working children who understood respect and honor. My mother didn't give me wealth, but she gave me valuable tools in how to be a woman who is strong, faithful, honest, knowledgeable, loving and a force of nature. Thank you, mom, for the treasure you poured into me.

## Chapter 3
### *What Is Family?*

This morning the idea of family is very heavy on my mind. God created family way back in the book of Genesis after he removed Adam and Eve from the garden. God removed them after they had fallen into disobedience before God, as disobedience (rebellion) is a sin. The new couple began to build a life outside of the garden and started their family. This family would be the of the first community. Family is the first human community God created.

What is the dictionary definition of Family? Family is defined as a clan, dynasty and species. Some synonyms of the word family are; domestic, household, personal, intimate, private and every day.

**A family is:**

1) A group of relatives

2) People who live together

3) A lineage

4) Offspring

5) A group of people with something in common

The previous definitions were taken right out of the American Dictionary and as you can see nowhere in the definitions does it say that a family is a group of people that are biologically related as linked by blood or birth order. A family is a group of individuals that truly love each other with no selfish intentions or benefits.

Let's look at this idea from a spiritual point of view. God has children that love Him and serve Him. However not all of God's created children are serving Him. God has many children that are estranged from Him and yet He still loves them too. A good case in point is the first biblical family in Genesis where we see the relationship of Able, Cain and the first couple themselves.

It is obvious that Adam taught his sons about God because both sons decided to bring God a sacrifice of their first fruits to God. The Bible tells us that God looked at Able's offering more favorably than that of Cain's. God never completely rejected Cain's sacrifice, but Cain felt slighted by God. Cain feeling slighted or rejected by God was yet another projection of Satan invading the first siblings.

## SINGLE ONE

This is where the family community faced their first challenge of grace, acceptance, and preference.

We assume that a family has built in emotional responses of positive total acceptance for their own but that is not necessarily true. Cain should have had an inborn familial acceptance for his brother Able but as we can read Cain's jealousy grew to the point that he was able to kill is brother. How is this possible?

We think that family is the one safe place we can trust however that is not true. Family can be the hardest community to be a part of.

Family can become jealous, vindictive, and violent towards their own when one person in that family outshines, out succeeds, or just has a grace about them that the others have not been blessed with.

I have learned in my own life, that it doesn't matter how much you love your family, protect them, care for them, shower them

## SINGLE ONE

with gifts, help them when they are in trouble or sacrifice for them. They will reject the one that has managed to outshine, outperform or has been given by no choice of their own, greater grace by God. Able did nothing to deserve what his brother did to him. It was not Able's intention to outshine his brother or out impress God, but Cain saw Able as a threat to his existence and he blamed Able for God's response. Was Cain right to feel the jealousy he felt, not at all? Cain should have gone to God and asked for guidance as to how to make his sacrifice more suitable to God.

In this era of complete selfishness, the loss of love (the word tells us in the last days the love of many will wax cold) self-promotion and the appetite for fame, a family can turn on the those who show forth unselfish behavior and real love.

I have seen this in my own life. Abandonment of family members towards one or two people in that family happens more often

## SINGLE ONE

than anyone can imagine. Those who you expect will love you no matter what will often walk away from you. Sometimes all it takes is you speaking truth, revealing or exposing a sin or refusing to keep God's word to yourself. Therefore, our first love has to be God. God tells us in His word that if we take up His cross and leave all others for Him, He will "surely take us up"; this means He will be our family. I have learned that those who love me unconditionally have one thing in common with me; the blood of the lamb has washed them. Jesus' blood ties us closer together than biology does. My greatest support has come from non-blood related people.

It's time to broaden your definition of family. Those who can and will love you unconditionally may not share the same blood or carry your last name.

I had to make God my all because the acceptance and pure love I needed, only He

## SINGLE ONE

was able to provide. I have no resentment towards my family nor do I reproach them when they happen to be around me. I have learned that the family community is subject to change so I do not put my trust in any person. People fail, family fails you, but God never fails us nor does He abandon those who love and serve Him. I have learned to lean into the God that loves and cares for me at all times not into my extended family. The joy we receive from God is that His blessings are poured out over all of those who have been abandoned by their loved ones. Jesus said, "Though your mother and father may abandon you the Lord your God will surely take you up." (Ps 27:10, Is. 49:15, Jer. 31:20)

For those who have been abandoned by their mothers and fathers God has a plan, which is that He desires to make you His child. God made man to long for human contact and it is this human contact that causes people to want to know who biologically created them.

## SINGLE ONE

There are others who have been adopted from birth and have no desire to ever meet their biological parents. These people have reported that the parents who adopted them had a choice to make and they chose to have a child they did not create to love. It is this miracle of love that compels them to never seek out their biological parents. Somehow, they have understood that having a person love them that did not have to is a much more powerful bond then that of random assignment.

SINGLE ONE

## Chapter 4

### *Not a Prophet Among your own Familial Rejection*

As soon as you understand who you are in Christ and begin walking in your purpose many around you will change their behavior towards you. Why does this happen so often?

Jesus Himself said, "There is no prophet without honor except those in their own house." (John 4:44, Luke 4:16-30) What does that mean?

## SINGLE ONE

1) The first people to deny who you are, are those in your own household. These are your own biological relatives as well as those of your own church.
2) The next group that may deny and reject who you are once you become who God as always meant for you to be are your friends and those in your circle
3) carnal minded people around you may not understand what and why God is doing what He is doing in you
4) even Jesus's own family, community and his own ethnic circle could not understand who He truly was. Jesus brothers joined Him after His ministry had started. Even Jesus' own family could not appreciate Him though they saw great miracles from Him.

We all assume that when God changes us and uses us that everyone we know will be happy for us but that is not always the case. Those around you may become jealous, question why you why not them? They may also question if what you

## SINGLE ONE

are doing for God is really God or you. This process can be very discouraging and can even cause some to be so hurt that they give up because they cannot handle the loss of people they care about. But my question is this, why would you want people to stay in your life who do not support or believe what God is doing in you, through you or with you?

Jesus did not concern Himself with His family's opinion about Him. At the age of twelve He broke away from His parents and went to the temple to discuss the word of God with adult Teachers and Scholars. They were shocked to see the level of knowledge and wisdom Jesus had at twelve. When His parents found Him after three days, His mother said, why have you done this? We have been looking for you for three days. Jesus answered her, "what do you want with me woman? Do you not know I have to be about my father's business?" In other words, I am not here to worry about my relationship with you I am here to carry out my Father's will on earth!

## SINGLE ONE

If God is using you and molding you don't worry about others. You are here on planet earth to carry out God's will not the will of others for you!

I had to come to this realization because there were many times that my own family refused to accept what God showed me about them, warnings of choices they were in danger of making and even the wrath of God to come. I gave my brother a word once that the girl he wanted to marry was not the one for him, and that if he married her she was going to cheat on him and there would be great suffering to come. The word also stated that his first child was going to be severely disabled. My brother rejected the word and so did his girlfriend. My mom came to me and said, "why are you always making trouble for this family?" Not even my mother supported the word of the Lord.

Well God never gets things wrong! My brother married the girl and she got pregnant less than a month after they were married. The baby was born blind, and severely handicapped, with full

## SINGLE ONE

blown diabetics, lack of moisture, no tear ducts and a brain that was facing the opposite direction so the only thing she could do was hear. My niece died at three and a half years old and is lying in a grave in Cypress Hills Cemetery in Brooklyn New York. The death added to the already bad relationship he had with his wife. Less than three years after his daughter's death, my brother's wife ran off with another man and left her younger daughter abandoned. My brother became a single father to a five-year-old little girl. Every word God spoke came to pass. My family was devastated. It has been twenty-six and a half years since my niece died and my brother has not gotten over it yet. A pain of this kind never leaves a person.

God tries so hard to keep us from suffering but for God to be successful in keeping us from such deep sorrow is that we must heed the warnings He sends us no matter who they come from.

I wish I could write that this was the only incident my family has suffered as a result of not

## SINGLE ONE

listening to God, but it is not. My extended family has had a great deal of tragedy but all of it has been attached to one fact, they will not accept the word of the Lord from my mouth. I have lived the verse "there is no prophet of honor in their own home." The pain I still feel even as I write these words go deep because nowhere in my heart would I ever want them to suffer as they have.

We must learn to be mature in our thinking of how and whom God can use to speak into our lives. If God could use a donkey to speak to Balaam (Numbers 22:28) and safe his life than God can use your family members to speak into yours.

Just in case a donkey is not around, here is a criterion for determining if a word is from God.

1) The person delivering the word should be a person of good testimony who is living for the Lord. They have good character and live a righteous life.

## SINGLE ONE

2) Not a gossiper who likes talking about others. Such people do not hear from God.

3) A safe approach is to know if the person is a prophet. Remember God will judge the word in the end and the prophet, and He punishes false prophets. We do not have to punish the false prophets!

4) The person stands nothing to gain from the word whether you follow it or not! (No jealousy or envy is present)

5) A non-prophet can have deep insight into a situation in your life and should not be discarded.

6) The person walks in wisdom and when they come to give you insight, they point out character issues in you but instead of hearing them out you ignore them or even get angry with them. This is a red flag that you are ignoring alarming behavior that God is trying to correct in you. People who demonstrate this type of behavior towards another are obviously rejecting

God's warnings and insight all together. One must wonder does this rejecter truly want to hear from God or is that something people say in church to fit in.

7) There are people that God gives very strong discernment to and can see into others. This gift has been around for thousands of years and it is not going away anytime soon. Discernment gives the person a word of knowledge. A word of knowledge is direct insight into a person's life whether in the present, past, or future.

Even if all the above statements are true about you people may still reject your advice. Be prepared for rejection, deflection, excuses and justifications as to why they are right, and you are wrong. When you give advice or a word from the Lord there will be people that no matter what God says, or people of wisdom say they are going to run ahead and do what they want to. People are largely insecure so if someone makes

*SINGLE ONE*

them feel good, happy or content in any way they will choose that person no matter what horrible character flaws are present.

**Serious Character flaws not to be ignored**: Lying, stealing, fraud, unfaithfulness, being in love with someone else's spouse, leading a double life, a violent temper, argumentative, failure to admit they are ever wrong, dishonoring your opinion ideas and values. They are financially irresponsible. They may also dislike your family or hate them completely. They dislike or hate your friends. They are demeaning and dismissive of your concerns, ideas, and hurts. They are demeaning of women/men and dismissive of women in power. These behaviors are very serious and if they are present in any relationship to any degree, rest assured that with time they will escalate in frequency. You have been warned. Take heed least you fall!!!

## Chapter 5
### *Leave Your Family!*

Luke 14:26 "Jesus said, if anyone come to me and does not hate his own father and mother and wife and children and brothers and sisters, yes and even his own life, he cannot be my disciple." This verse is highly controversial for some but in accordance with God's word, it is the expectation of God for our relationship with God in order that it may

## SINGLE ONE

function correctly. In order to follow Jesus, we must like the Apostles, be willing to leave behind our familial circles. This leaving behind of the familial circle indicates to the Lord that we have chosen Him first over all others. Many today still cannot do this and therefore lack a deep and intimate relationship with God because they are yet to make Him their all in all.

Is Jesus telling us it is okay to hate others? No, He is not! What Jesus is saying is that if you are not willing to forsake others to follow God then you are not worthy of Him. We cannot say we love God but are not willing to follow God over others.

I have seen people follow their family into destruction and then wonder why they are so unhappy and suffering. I have seen others follow their friends over God and ignore God's chosen leaders to make their friends feel supported. God will never ask you to turn your back on your Pastor without solid concrete evidence of sin in the person. Not gossip not second or third had information from someone who is bitter or angry

## SINGLE ONE

with the Pastor because they didn't get their way on an issue. God has called us to follow Him and if we cannot choose Him then we make ourselves unworthy of Him altogether.

There are families that are so toxic to each other that their presence in your life is counterproductive to your growth. There are families that are so involved in evil, crime and criminal activities that you really must walk away from them just so you do not get caught up in their web of crime and lies.

When I was a little girl my mom kept my siblings and I away from certain family members. Why? Because they were doing drugs and selling drugs. One relative even made the following statement, "I am going to introduce drugs into this entire family and to every cousin I have." Once my mom got wind of this statement my mom stopped going over to see them and they never came to our house either. This may seem harsh but as a mother I can understand why she took such drastic measures to keep us safe. My mom had

## SINGLE ONE

determined that no one was going to ruin us. I am very glad my mom took this position on my behalf. There were other relatives who did not keep their children away from that individual and as a result they lost children to overdoses. This did not need to happen to my cousins! Some family members should not have access to your loved ones.

What are you resolving to do to keep God first in your life? Have you resolved to make all necessary changes in your life so that you are following God and not others? To keep God first we must make a resolution to ourselves to this effect. What is a resolution then?

A resolution is a determined decision to bring about an outcome that is beneficial and accomplishes a significant milestone. A person cannot make a resolution unless they have a resolute attitude, mind and heart.

A resolute mind is one that is unwavering, unmovable, determined, steadfast and unstoppable. In order to accomplish anything in

## SINGLE ONE

life or for the Lord we have to have a made-up resolute mind, heart and behavior. Your behavior demonstrates the strength and firmness of your mind.

Who may you have to pull away from in order to make God first? We must keep God first so that no other idols take His place.

1) Prayer helps us make God first everyday
2) Devotional time of worship helps us keep God first
3) Fellowship in the house of God (attending church is a must)
4) Surrounding yourself with people who pray for you as well
5) Remove yourself from toxic family members and situations
6) Protect your mind, heart, and life
7) Pour the word of God into your spirit

The word of God calls us to be strong in the Lord. **I Corinthians 15:58** "Therefore, my beloved brethren, be steadfast, immovable, always

## SINGLE ONE

abounding in the work of the Lord, knowing that your labor is not in vain in the Lord."

We are to be steadfast in our heart concerning all things of God but also concerning our lives. We were created in the image of God, Jesus and the Holy Spirit. They are our firm foundation and solid rock!

It's time to be firm, strong in God and in His purpose for our lives! Stop thinking about what He wants you to do and start walking in it, living in it and remaining in it!

## Chapter 6
### *Get Rid of Sin*

Psalms 66:18 "If I regard iniquity in my heart then the Lord will not hear."

To regard iniquity means to hold that sin in high esteem. It means I admire and hold that sin in a respectful way in my life even though I know it's a sin. The word iniquity means sin or wickedness that is harmful to your life, soul, heart and mind. Iniquity is also a strong hold (a sinful act) that

## SINGLE ONE

the person struggles with and repeats often. The word iniquity can also represent hate or resentment against someone. The verse tells us that if we are keeping iniquity in our heart then the Lord will not hear us.

What is it that God will not hear?
God will not hear our prayers, our cry, our petitions, and our request. Why should He?

God requires a heart that is free of sin, anger and resentment. All anger, hatred, resentment and sin keep God from hearing our prayers and needs!

Are you causing God not to hear you? Is your heart condition keeping your promises and prayers from coming to pass?

Your remedy is to go before God and ask Him to remove all hate, resentment, and wickedness against anyone out of your heart. God is able to cleanse forgive and forget your offenses, but others also need forgiveness as well.

## SINGLE ONE

Why should God forgive you if you can't forgive anyone?

Get your prayers answered, empty your heart of all hindrances!

**What forgiveness is not?**

1) Forgiveness is not excusing a person's bad behavior
2) Forgiveness is not pretending the bad behavior never happened
3) Forgiveness is not ignoring what happened
4) Forgiveness is not keeping toxic people in your life

**What forgiveness is?**

1) Forgiveness is you choosing to let go of the right to punish someone who has wronged you
2) Forgiveness is showing mercy to an undeserving person

## SINGLE ONE

3) Forgiveness is letting go of the offense so you can heal

4) Forgiveness is acting like Christ and giving forgiveness to others who hurt you and do not deserve forgiveness. Christ did this for humanity.

5) Forgiveness is ridding yourself of the burden of anger and resentment

6) When you let go of the resentment you are able to enjoy life with joy

7) Forgiveness is a choice

Too many people are walking around injured by others with open wounds. What I have found is that the injured person is bleeding out on the person or persons who injured them and are living their life with no concern for the injured at all. People think that those who injure are remorseful. Truly toxic people lack remorse and empathy. Those who walk around hurt and mournful about their injuries are expending

## SINGLE ONE

energy on situations and others who aren't losing sleep over it at all.

I have seen people hold on to their bitterness and injury to the point of making themselves sick. No one person or person's is worth you becoming sick, losing your mind or living a life void of joy. Stop giving your life and joy away for hopeless causes. Jesus said it best "For if **ye forgive** men their trespasses, your heavenly. Father will also **forgive you**: But if **ye forgive** not men their, trespasses, neither will your Father **forgive** your trespasses. Matthew 6:14,15

God's word holds true forever. If we forgive, we are making an investment in our own future. We will need forgiveness one day too and isn't it comforting to know that we can go to God and ask forgiveness and will not be denied!

I have suffered a lot of persecution at the hands of many ignorant, mean, evil and jealous people. Just imagine if I had carried around all the hurt

## SINGLE ONE

from when I was five (my first hurt) till now (59) I would be a miserable, empty basket case of a person. I would be completely useless to my family, friends, and God's people. But I choose to walk in the liberty of heart, mind, and spirit by choosing to let go and forgive.

## Chapter 7
### *Trust*

The Lord reminds us that we are to "cast off all worry."

The word cast off means to push away, to put away, to remove, to dispose of, to expel from, to eliminate something that is annoying or that is harmful to health, mind, or spirit!

The word instructs us to cast off our worry.

## SINGLE ONE

Why? Because when we worry, we have stepped out of trusting in the Lord and have taken on the responsibility of trying to determine how to solve our own situations. When we worry, we are causing ourselves harm. We know that medical science has linked worry and stress to numerous diseases like heart disease, thyroid failure, high blood pressure and even diabetes. Worry can also cause unnecessary anxiety that leads to sleeplessness and put you in the hospital for mental disorders.

The word tells us "casting our cares on Him for He cares for you." When we cast our cares on the Lord, He uses His strength the strength we do not have, and He establishes the form and time for how He will help us with all our burdens.

Trust in the Lord to carry you and all your burdens!

What does trust in God mean to you?

Trust is defined as the firm belief, reliability ability or strength in someone or something.

## SINGLE ONE

To trust in God means you firmly believe in His ability to bring about what He has promised you.

Trust also means that the person you are trusting in has the ability to deliver because He is reliable. To be a reliable person means that you have successfully proven to others that you can be depended on because you have come through for them before. God can be relied on because He comes through for His children repeatedly. He never fails nor can He be out done by anyone else.

We can trust God because He is our strong tower into which we can run into for refuge but also for strength. God is a mighty God whose strength is unmatched and because it's unmatched no one can conquer Him. No one can outwit God, out plan Him or outperform His mighty works ever. He stands alone in His power; therefore, we can trust Him.

As children we must remind ourselves that the God that is orchestrating our lives relies on His wisdom, His knowledge, His own understanding

## SINGLE ONE

that cannot be matched by human intellect! God and God alone will accomplish what He has told you He will do! God is sovereign and to be sovereign means that God is the ultimate authority. He is supreme, outstanding and ruler of all things. To be sovereign means that God is self-governing which means He governs Himself and man can never order Him around. God is self-determining which means He determines His own mind without counsel from anyone. In Job chapter 40 we can read how God confronts Job and asks him a series of questions. God ask Job where were you when I laid the foundation of the earth, and the entire universe? Where were you Job when I separated the seas, when I put the stars in their place and called them by name? Where were you Job when I decided where to store all snow, thunder, and lighting. To be sovereign means that God has complete power and is the Master all the earth, mankind, and every creature He has created.

God has been around for an eternity and He is all

## SINGLE ONE

knowledge, wisdom and understanding. We cannot possibly believe that we know what is best for our life's over what God's plans are for our us. Is it not time for you to let go and let God direct your life? Tap into God's wisdom by allowing Him to direct your path and put your life in order.

## Chapter 8
## *Courtship/Dating*

Some years ago Oprah had woman on her show that wrote a book called "How to Get Him to Marry you in a Year". The woman had been an avid dater who was very used to dating a man a couple of times and then going to bed with him. Well this left her empty and alone. She decided to become celibate. The woman decided

## SINGLE ONE

to go back to the way things used to be. She decided to let men she met know that she was not going to bed with them and that she was waiting to marry to resume having sex again. At first the woman said that men would end the date never to call her again. But in just a few more months she met a man that respected what she was doing, and she began dating him or courting him. He never went to her apartment and she never went to his apartment. They went to the movies, talked, museums, parks, and jazz clubs and went for long walks. They really talked and began to get to know each other's likes, dislikes, dreams, victories and failures. They became real friends. Six months after they met, he proposed. She was ready because they spent their time getting to know each other and did not cloud their senses by lust. She felt respected and he admired her greatly. Exactly one year later they were married and years later they still are. Many women ran out and bought the book and many began courting instead of dating men. There were many marriages that proceeded out

## SINGLE ONE

of those who bought into the idea of courting. I was stunned by Oprah's response to the woman. "You mean to tell me that you have gone back to if you want milk you have to buy the cow first." I was disappointed with Oprah who I happen to admire greatly. But Oprah's response represents the overall opinion of the culture at large.

Courting is what many think is an outdated process however as the author proved in her own life men are looking for women that are more chase. Men may want to sleep around with a loose woman, but they want to take a good girl home to meet mom. Keeping yourself pure until marriage is an excellent and good move.

1) You do not have to worry about sexually transmitted diseases
2) Saving oneself allows for the couple to really get to know each other
3) Fear of pregnancy is gone
4) The couple grows in love over lust

## SINGLE ONE

5) Lust fizzles out over time but love is forever
6) You don't have to walk in shame or guilt
7) You don't have to sit by the phone waiting for that guy to call you back
8) Men respect women who respect themselves
9) Keeping yourself builds up good anticipation
10) Waiting until marriage does not allow soul ties or demonic entities to follow you home. Demonic entities can attach themselves to people via sexual intercourse. Sexual intercourse is a spiritual act, but I will address that later.

Dating is not what it used to be, but you don't have to follow the crowd! You can determine to keep yourself. Try courting!

The unsaved are trying courting now as well. So, what is courting?

## SINGLE ONE

1) Going out to public places but never looking to be alone with a guy or girl
2) Going out in a group or with another couple
3) No liquor when you are together/ if saved you shouldn't be drinking anyway
4) Setting a time limit when out for example 7pm-10pm depending on the activity
5) Accountability partners must help especially if you are feeling weak in the knees
6) Don't be afraid to tap out and cancel if you are having real bad lust feelings
7) Talk, talk, talk
8) Ask important questions about family size, financial practices, health issues within your family and his

The culture encourages men and woman to engage in sex to connect with someone but, sex can separate a couple. Why should a man ride you first as if you were a car? How many rides do

## SINGLE ONE

you have to entertain before you become a used car? If given the choice of a new car or a used car which car would you want to drive? I have heard so many stories from women/men that have engaged in frequent sex with different partners only to be left feeling empty and unloved. No one who truly loves you would want you to feel used. Human beings are not animals. Animals engage in sex to procreate. Yet there are animals that show love for life to each other. Eagles, penguins, cranes, gray wolves, bald eagles, Gibbon (ape), Beavers and even vultures' mate for life that is a whole lot better than humans themselves. Don't be worse than an animal! You can exercise self-control while at the same time building a real loving relationship with someone.

## Chapter 9
### *What makes for a good relationship?*

I met my husband on a blind date thirty-four years ago. This meeting was not by chance but by God's divine providence. God started working on my encounter with my husband when I was eighteen years old. I worked with a missionary in Coney Island NY the summer before I started college. At the end of this amazing experience

## SINGLE ONE

the missionary prophet gave me a word. She said "God has chosen your husband for you. He will come from Puerto Rico and when he and you are ready (when God's plan was ready) God will bring this to pass!"

You would think I would be happy but I wasn't.

1) I had not prayed about a husband since I was like ten after I heard a sermon in church

2) I had a five year plan for my BS and MS degree, then a job then maybe I would settle down

3) I DID NOT WANT A LATINO MAN

4) I did not want a man from Puerto Rico

When I angrily told my mom what the prophet told me she gave me some powerful words of wisdom:

"Lydia why are you upset? That prophecy is a future prophecy. God knows you are going to school because He told you to go. You must take that word write it out and put it in your jewelry box and let God fulfill it in His time. When you

## SINGLE ONE

are ready by God's measurement not yours it will come to pass!"

Mom was right! I wrote it out and put it away. Seven years later God's word walked into my life. God had to work on me for eight years, removing stuff from my heart and doing a work in my life.

Just because you can cook, clean, work, sew, dress, sing and are charming and intelligent doesn't mean your insides are ready for marriage. Inside work takes longer!

So, if you want God to give you a hubby ask yourself and God this:

Are my insides (heart, spirit, emotions, mind, character, personality, attitudes and painful experiences) ready for a deep intimate and committed marriage?

When I met my husband 34 years ago, I had no idea that I would be marrying him two years later. It was not love at first sight for me, but I felt drawn to him as if I had known him for years and had been separated for a time and now, we were finally coming back together. When my husband Chris started talking about spending the rest of his life with me, I arranged for us to have a sit down where we could discuss our mutual non-negotiables for the relationship. I had to know what he considered issues or behaviors that would end the relationship. Neither of us wanted to go into the relationship with the idea of divorce as an option. We both worked on our list for a week and came together on a Saturday to discuss them with each other.

**Lydia's List of non-negotiables**

1) Unfaithfulness of any kind (physical, emotional, or financial) would not be tolerated.

A) Physical unfaithfulness includes all forms of sex oral or otherwise

B) Emotional unfaithfulness is turning to another man or woman and sharing with them personal information about your relationship where you complain about your husband

## SINGLE ONE

C) Financial cheating is taking money, trips, jewelry, vacations, or any other material goods from another person outside the marriage and your spouse does not know about it.

2) Abuse of any kind including verbal, physical, emotional (manipulation, tricks, undermining) Psychological and financial

3) No name calling (skinny, fatty, stupid, or worst ECT.)

4) No lying to each other

5) Failure to protect your spouse from your family and friends (not everyone in a family will love your spouse but that does not give them the right to talk about them to you, pick on them, or demean them in anyway) Your family will protect your spouse if they see you protecting them.

6) Jealousy has no place in a marriage. Personally, I see it as a sign of insecurity. A spouse should never express jealousy towards their spouse if their partner is prospering. I

made more money than my husband did for the first twelve years of our marriage and my husband always addressed this way; "Who cares who can buy more bacon in the home. We will both fry it up and eat it just the same."

7) Do not allow family or friends to borrow money or ask for money repeatedly from you. It creates terrible blood between everyone.

8) No hiding money from each other. This includes raises, promotions, bonuses, inheritance, lottery winning or increases or any kind.

9) No purchasing of large ticket items without your spouse knowing it.

10) All major financial decisions are made together

11) Family planning is done together

12) No impeding each other from practicing faith

I am not sharing my husband's list because when we sat down and I took out my list, his list was the same. This is when I knew without any

## SINGLE ONE

doubts that we were going to make it as a couple. I am blessed to report that in 32 years we have followed our list and adjusted as we changed, jobs changed, I retired and our children came, but the foundation of our relationship has remained strongly rooted in God, His word and our list. Don't you dare marry anyone until you make up your non-negotiable list!

## Chapter 10
### *A good man not a perfect man*

What makes for a good man? For most women, the example of a good man is usually their father or grandfather. I will attempt to share what attributes make for a good man. Let's look at what the word attribute actually means. An attribute is a quality, a characteristic, trait, feature point, aspect, or element. An attribute can be physical, emotional, or

## SINGLE ONE

psychological ways a person responds to others or in a situation.

**A Good Man Traits**

1) Loving
2) Honesty, trust worthiness (share faith with)
3) Compassionate
4) Hardworking
5) Committed
6) Humorous
7) Understanding
8) Honorable
9) Faithful
10) Kind
11) Fair
12) Patient
13) Smart
14) Industrious, humble, reliable

Please notice that I did not include handsome or drop dead gorgeous to the list of attributes because for a while I only dated good-looking guys. Well God took care of that too. You see every good-looking guy I dated turned out to be real jerks, self-centered and selfish. I had to learn the hard way, that how the book looked on the outside did not give me the full picture of what was truly on the inside.

## SINGLE ONE

My dad personally had many of these attributes, but he lacked faithfulness to my mom. He cheated on her many times and that truly destroyed trust in my mom and made her insecure in their relationship (I lost my dad 10 years ago and I lost mom 5 years ago). My dad's behavior affected me deeply. Dads are the first relationship a girl has with a man and it will make or break a girl's perception of what a good relationship looks like. For me my dad's behavior made me become distrusting of all men. I truly believed that all men were unable of being faithful. My dad's behavior created a deep anger in me that manifested itself in my desire not to allow any man to dominate me in anyway. If I perceived a man was trying to tell me what to do, that was enough for me to break off the relationship. This anger and resentment followed me into my relationship. I projected this anger and distrust onto my husband though he had nothing to do with my dad's behavior. My husband never demonstrated any behavior that

## SINGLE ONE

would lead me to believe he would be or was in anyway like my dad. For me to develop a healthy relationship with my husband, I had to come to the realization that my dad had failed me.

It wasn't until the summer of 1997 after leaving a women's seminar with my former boss that my truth about my dad finally came out. It was a statement by my former boss that un-leached it all. She said to me, "my dad was a tumble weed but I still loved him!" I asked her what that meant exactly, and she told me her dad had been a cheat. It was then that I shared my truth. As I cried telling her about my dad's repeated indiscretions I felt as though all the years of hidden pain and embarrassment was leaving my body. I became free when I told my truth. It was no longer a family secret I kept hidden from everyone. You see my dad was a Minister, Evangelist, Prophet and then a Pastor. When he was living for the Lord he was on fire and no one could touch him, but when he would back slide (leave the church and God) he became a

## SINGLE ONE

cheating, lying and adulterous man. All the years of carrying around his shame was released in one car ride from Jamaica way in Boston to Cambridge where I lived. When I got home, I tearfully told my husband who my daddy truly was all of it, the great, the bad and the ugly. That one afternoon set me free and it was then and there I began to trust my husband for the first time.

Pay close attention to the attributes of your dad or grandfather they matter greatly!

Do not opt to take on another persons' problems if you cannot carry your own! People by and large do not change unless confronted with the impending loss of life, lively hold or family. And even then, some people still choose not to change. I saw my mom struggle for decades desiring for my father's cold ways to change. It never happened. People who truly do not want to change will not. Therefore, I advise all who are reading this book to pay attention to the character qualities and flaws you are drawn to.

**SINGLE ONE**

You may think you can handle a person's flaws when you will exhaust yourself trying and rob yourself of peace and joy in the end!

## Chapter 11
### *A good woman not a perfect one*

Too often men are misled by a woman's looks. Men are very visual and rely on what they see to determine attraction. While no one can truly speak for what individual men are attracted to it is a scientific fact that men are very much led by their eyes when it comes to women. Just as women must have an idea of what qualities they look for in a man, men also

## SINGLE ONE

must pay close attention to a woman's character over her looks. After all, beauty fades with time but a person's character will last for a life-time.

Here are just some qualities that a man should consider when choosing a spouse. Some of these character traits are those my husband shared with me. I respect his opinion as a man and as a man who took many things into consideration before he asked me to marry him.

**A Good Woman: My husband told me I took you to meet my family and you were the only girl I did that with. I had never deemed any other girl I had previously met worthy to meet my family.**

1) Loving

2) Intelligent

3) Kind

4) A good homemaker

5) A friend

6) Successful

7) Hard working

## SINGLE ONE

8) Supports your dreams without jealousy

9) Someone you would want to raise children with

10) Good with money

11) Physically beautiful to me

12) Men like to eat so learn how to cook

13) Understanding

14) Able to share dreams and goals with

15) Honorable, honest, moral, faithful

16) Family oriented

These attributes are by no means the only list a man should have but they are a good start. Some men may want a woman who shares some of his interest like, exercising, camping, fishing, animation or even building things. Men love to do physical things with their spouse, because they want to keep the same energy they had in the relationship when they were dating. A man likes to continue to date his wife even after they are married. My husband still enjoys going out with me. Whether it's going to the movies, museums, mini golfing, amusement parks, river rafting, shopping, redecorating our home or praying he loves spending time with me. Men have a real need to know and experience shared time with their spouse. Men want to feel proud of having the woman of their dreams with them because a wife truly becomes her husband's best friend.

In choosing a mate a person must consider all aspects of a person's character. Ignoring serious character issues can open the person up to a world of hurt, a lifetime of regrets and unnecessary situations. Ask God for direction in choosing a mate it will save you from a great deal of disaster.

**A closing thought**: Always know what is happening financially in your home. Never rely solely on your husband to manage, handle, and run all the finances including filling taxes, paying bills or loaning anyone any money. Women have suffered great lost because they became lazy about knowing what's going on financially in

## SINGLE ONE

their homes. Don't be lazy or ignorant about what's going on with your household's money. Stay informed! Know what outstanding debt you have, life insurance, bonds, 401k accounts and retirement plans. We must trust our spouse intelligently but not be blind to our financial life!

## Chapter 12
### *Building a Healthy Family Structure*

How do you build a family structure that is spiritually and emotionally healthy? Your first step is to establish a relationship where God is first in your life.

1) A couple must first establish norms for their own relationship first. What are our relationship goals? What are our boundaries as a couple?

## SINGLE ONE

2) A Family should be an extension of your relationship. Faith, Love, respect, trust, safety, security, honesty, purity (in the individuals and in relationship), kindness, personal responsibility and cooperation are all norms on which a family must be built. These create a healthy environment where children and adults can thrive.

3) Having shared memories! Children will remember some of what you say but they remember 100% of what you do with them and what they see. Be a good example!

4) How you treat your spouse in front of your children is how they will treat each other and their spouses in the future!

5) Make time for your spouse! Make time for your children and laugh together!

6) Teach children to be responsible by assigning chores. Teach financial responsibility by showing them how to save for something they would like. Children who are taught financial responsibility grow up to be financially responsible adults who know

## SINGLE ONE

how to manage their finances!

7) If you want peace in your home then you must be a peacemaker in your home!

8) Whether you are a believer or not the fact remains true. Families need to bond, and faith is a great place where families can come together and share a spiritual bond. Faith is very important for children it gives them a moral compass and grounds them to something greater them themselves.

Building a healthy family means that great consideration must be given to mental health as well. Guarding one's mental health is important to personal and spiritual peace. How does a person guard their mental health?

1) Make time for meditation, or quiet time in prayer

2) Read the bible, or self-help books that can serve as tools to guide you

## SINGLE ONE

3) Exercise is an excellent way to clear the mind it also helps you lose weight

4) The brain chemicals released during exercise endorphins create a feeling of well being

5) Surround yourself with people who are encouraging

6) Music can be a great stress releaser

7) Make sure you are getting enough sleep

8) Disconnect from technology and enjoy nature for a change of pace

9) Stop yelling in your home. Speak in calm voices. Peace brings peace!

10) If you have a pet go for a walk or play with your pet it also promotes calmness

May God help you all as you establish firm foundations that will sustain your families as they grow!

## Chapter 13
### *Real Marriage Talk*

There are many of you that want a husband or a wife. As a married woman of 32 years there is something you need to know about marriage.

## SINGLE ONE

**Ladies:**

1) He is not going to take you out to dinner every night
2) Learn to cook its cheaper than take out or eating out
3) He is not going to hire a maid
4) Learn to clean with real cleaning products! Bleach is a friend!
5) He will want sex on the nights you are most tired so rest when you can
6) They need sex like they need oxygen
7) Keep your mom, her ideas and opinions out of your marriage. He married you not your mom! Keep all your family members out of your marriage!
8) Don't nag! They hate that! Plus, you're not his mom!
9) Don't flirt with anyone because he will never trust you again!

## SINGLE ONE

10) Tell him you admire him and how hard he works to provide. They love to hear that!

11) Watch a movie he likes it will not kill you

12) Share in an activity he enjoys and helps to build intimacy

13) Tell him he's smart when he is!

14) Let him be a father to his kids. He made half of them anyway plus you get a break. Be smart!

**Gents:**

1) She is not going to have sex with you everywhere you guys go!

2) She is not going to sleep in a sexy nighty every night but if she does it's on!

3) Foreplay begins in the morning if you want sex in the evening

4) Listen to comprehend not because she wants you to fight her battles

5) Admire her strength and notice her haircuts, color changes and style

## SINGLE ONE

6) Be honest but not brutal
7) Buy her something in her style she will know you are paying attention
8) Keep your mom and family out of her business
9) Your mom isn't going to sleep with you so defend her against family and don't let them talk bad about her in your presence. This will show your family you respect her, and they will respect her as well
10) Watch a movie she likes it won't kill you
11) Vacuum a rug. Women love it when a man helps! Sex will happen
12) If you are wrong, admit to it right away and there will be no arguments
13) When children come, she will not want to have sex if the door is not locked tight!

Marriage requires hard work. People believe that once you're married just having sex is all that is needed to keep things on track in a relationship.

## SINGLE ONE

Not so! Marriage requires patience, trust and forgiveness. There are times when you want to respond to your mate in a rude way or in a sarcastic manner, don't do it. I have learned that the best word is the one that you do not say at all. Not every remark requires a response. There are times your spouse will say something you do not like but you must weigh your response. You must learn not to sweat the small stuff. For a conversation to go array it requires two people to argue and blow things out of portion. Women especially are more prone to overreact and become too emotional over things they do not have to become emotional about. I have found it best to take a pause before responding and consider your responses before speaking.

Practicing the pause is a way to head off a bad interaction before it gets out of hand. This pause can be counting in your mind till ten or twenty before opening your mouth to respond.

I hope this insight will help you because they have helped me for 32 years and counting!

## Chapter 14

### *If two would agree/Two are better than one*

God always fulfills His promises! The word tells us 2 Peter 3:9 "For the Lord is not slack concerning His promises, as some men count slackness but is long suffering towards us; not willing that any should perish but that all should come to repentance."

## SINGLE ONE

This word has been tested in my lifetime and time again. When our family was living in Cambridge, Massachusetts we had a preacher come to our church home and the preacher invited my husband and I up when he was praying for people. I do not go up for prayer unless the Lord calls me because I do not like to chase words from prophets like some do. Nevertheless, my husband and I were obedient, and we went to the altar when we were called up. The preacher began to speak into our lives the following: "God is telling you that you will settle here for a while. As a matter of fact, God is going to give you a house." As I stood there with my husband, I had an immediate thought. I said to myself "I never asked God for a house." No sooner had I had this thought then the preacher says to me, "Lydia if God wants to give you a house why would you questions that? God knows you didn't ask Him for a house, but He wants to give you one. Is that okay with you?" Well I was so embarrassed in that moment because the

## SINGLE ONE

preacher through God's revelation had read my heart in the immediate moment.

My husband and I began looking for houses the following month even though we had no money saved up for a down payment. We decided to also pray together about what specific things we needed in a house. We also prayed for the neighborhood, a good school system and for the house not to be too far from our church. My husband and I must have looked at 100 houses over the course of three years. We were just about to give up searching at all. Then on Memorial Day weekend I went to church with our sons and my husband said he would meet us there. The entire service had gone by and no sign of my husband. I was so angry with him. Just when the closing prayer was going forth the door opens in the back and in walks my husband. I looked at him with an angry stare. My husband rushed over to me and quickly said to me honey I found a house. I thought to myself, "what you found a house without me?" He grabbed me by

## SINGLE ONE

the arm and walked over to the pastor to explain why he had missed the entire service. Our pastor being an understanding man told him I completely understand Chris, no worries. My in-laws were in town, so we asked them if they

would take the boys to lunch and then back to our apartment while Chris and I went to look at this house he found. When I get into my husband's car, he begins to tell me the whole story.

"Honey I left our apartment to come to church, but a voice kept telling me Chris keep driving so I did. I got on highway 93 and I kept driving until I saw a sign come up with a little community called Reading. I heard that voice tell me get off here, turn here turn there and I did. When I stopped, I was in front of a house and the real estate agent was taking down the open house sign. I asked her if I could have a look. I proceeded to follow her into the house, and

## SINGLE ONE

something happened." Just then we arrived at the house, but he told me we could finish the conversation later. I looked at the white little house with the black shutters and said, "This house is too small!" My husband told me honey give it a chance. You have to see the inside first before you make a judgment. My husband led the way. By the time my husband took me back to the house the agent was gone so we had to ask the owners if we could take a look at the house. Well just as I stepped over the threshold, I heard a small voice whisper to me "You are home!" I was stunned because the house was poorly furnished; the front living room was crowded with computers so I could not appreciate the lay out. I noticed a small corner sticking out from behind a computer and asked if there was a fireplace behind it. There was a lovely fireplace with a wonderful mantle. We then walked through the small kitchen into the grand ballroom as I called it. You see the owner had added 1,100 additional feet to the house creating a huge ballroom that was an additional living

## SINGLE ONE

room with an old fashion wood burning stove in addition to a master suite with its own entrance and master bath downstairs. It was a cape style house that had been expanded. The ballroom was gorgeous. The house had a first-floor bathroom and two large bedrooms on the second floor with an additional full bathroom. The house was larger on the inside then it let on, on the outside. When my husband took me downstairs to look at the bedroom, I shared with him what the voice had told me when I walked in. Well it was then that my husband confessed that the same thing had happened to him. Therefore, he insisted I go with him to see the house he wanted God to confirm it to me as well. Well I said now we have to negotiate because God told me "we are not going to pay full price for this house." God was working everything out for us. As my husband and the lady's boyfriend talked the lady and I became acquainted.

As the lady (Frances) and I talked I learned she had been a teacher and had left the profession

## SINGLE ONE

and was now selling medical equipment, making more money with very little stress. She also told me that she had found a house in Colorado and they only had one month to sell the house because her other closing was in June. She also told me that forty people had come through the house, but no one had shown any interest at all. She also told me her hubby was not a hubby but a boyfriend and his name was not on the deed. This was probably why the house was not properly furnished and the front room was a computer business. Well God allowed this woman to open up to me completely because God was setting us up for the sales pitch. All of sudden my husband to talk about the master bedroom's lay out. I shared with him there was a ledge that went all the way around the bedroom. He of course had not noticed it at all. So, we went back down to the master bedroom for a second look. It was then I shared all the information Frances had shared with me.

## SINGLE ONE

My husband said to me then this is what we will do. I will make them an offer. I reminded him that we had to make an offer below what they were asking for because it was what God had told me. So back upstairs we went. We asked for a piece of paper to write our offer on. They provide a piece of paper. My husband wrote the offer out folded it and gave it to Frances. She opened it and was visibly disappointed with the amount. The boyfriend took the paper and began to object to the offer. My husband equipped with all the info I had given him said to the boyfriend, "I am sorry, but I cannot negotiate with you because your name is not on the deed. I can only negotiate with Frances as the only legal owner of this house." (My husband is a corporate attorney) The man was visibly agitated, but he could not do anything about it. We left the residence and gave them our phone number. When my husband and I got into our car he told me "well it's up to God now."

## SINGLE ONE

We drove back to Cambridge and exactly twenty minutes after arriving at our apartment our home phone rang it was Frances. She was accepting our offer and wanted to know if we could come back to the house to sign a purchase agreement offer. We quickly backtracked to Reading and a half hour later we were signing a purchasing agreement. The process of buying our first home had just begun.

God had kept His promise to us. We had found the right house; with all the details we had asked Him for, in a great school system and only twelve miles from our church and jobs. We also paid less for a huge house with the biggest driveway, a three-season room, a huge basement, washer and dryer and a wraparound porch on a tree-lined street. God also made it possible for us to move in right after school let out and still enjoyed the summer with the kids with plenty of time for them to start in their new school. God had laid out every detail for us and made sure the house purchase worked for us all. Frances

## *SINGLE ONE*

got her house too and did not lose her beautiful new house in Colorado.

God knows how long we can wait for His promises to arrive. God knows exactly when and how to make things work out for our good and His glory. We must though agree with our spouses if we want God to bring His blessings into our lives. Do not give up because He is faithful unlike any other person! Some give up inches from their promises not realizing God's word was so close to them. Don't do that! Tough it out! Show God just how much trust you have in Him and He will show you just how faithful He is!!!

## Chapter 15
### *Real Love*

Women and men often make the mistake of interpreting lust for love. Lust is an emotional response coupled with a physical reaction. The brain during lust becomes flooded with endorphin chemicals equal to a drug dose. This chemical reaction is quick and can last for months every time you see or are with the person you are attracted to. However, as

## SINGLE ONE

powerful as lust may feel it is not love. Just because your brain reacts to a stimulant doesn't mean you are in love. Lust fades with time sometimes within months, as was the case for me. I never dated anyone longer than eight months because his appeal would wear off. The lust had turned itself off. Funny thing is that as the lust turned off, I would begin to see all the guys' flaws, which were always there, it's just that lust had blinded me from seeing the true person. Real love is not temporary, and it does not turn itself off.

Women and men must truly examine the feelings they have for each other. Therefore, abstaining from sex is the best option.

### Abstaining From Sex:

1) Allows you to get to know the person without letting your emotions to get in the way
2) Allows for people to see each other clearly and examine each other's

## SINGLE ONE

3) character traits without lust getting in the way

4) Still allows for attraction but keeps out of fornication

5) Doesn't open the door to soul ties in your life

6) Soul ties are spiritual bonds that form when couples have sex

7) People are spirit beings and can carry good and evil spirits within themselves unknowingly

8) Sleeping around exposes you to evil spirits from others that are transmitted through sex

9) Sexual intercourse is a spiritual act created by God as a way for a man and a woman to become one in spirit. Sex is a spiritual bond! It is a powerful experience that if had within the holy bonds of marriage becomes spiritual and entirely

## SINGLE ONE

different from having sex for lustful purposes.

God created love as a spiritual connection between a man and a woman where they can become on. Why did God go through the trouble of creating such a powerful emotion as love? Because God is love in action! God's love is not temporary but permanent.

**GOD'S LOVE:**

God's love is limitless! God has never set a limit to His love. We know this to be true because His word tells us in John 3:16 "For God so loved the world that He gave His only begotten Son that whosoever believes in Him will not perish but have everlasting life."

God spares no expense to bring mankind back into relationship with Him. Man was estranged from God so God pulled out all the stops and sent His Son as the only sacrifice pure enough to die in our place. Did we deserve this sacrifice?

## SINGLE ONE

Absolutely not! We had done nothing to receive such a priceless great gift from God. We deserved death and instead God sent life and love!

God did not stop at just forgiving us of our sins, or liberating us from the shame and guilt sin brings but He went one step further. God trumped Himself by also giving us power over death; the grave and He made eternal life available through His Son. We now can live a life in Him and also die in Him knowing that we do not die but merely sleep. This sleep is for the body alone because the spirit of man returns to God who gave it!

No human could ever purchase such gifts for only God has the heart big enough to give without reservation! What are you waiting for? Accept His love gift for your life.

SINGLE ONE

## Chapter 16
### *SEX, SEX, SEX*

God created sex! That's right God created sex for His children to enjoy within the boundaries He set up!

Genesis 2:18 tell us that "God saw Adam was alone and it was not good!" What did God see in Adam that was not good? Did He see Adam's frustration, loneliness, or did He see Adam's heart was missing something he needed?

## SINGLE ONE

Whatever God saw it was enough to move God to act. This action was the creation of Eve. Eve was God's comfort to Adam.

This comfort God provided gave way to Adam knowing Eve (sexually). This sexual encounter though was a spiritual covenant. God created this union as both a union of flesh and the spirit. Having sex outside of the boundaries of God's covenant does not diminish the power in the covenant but rather respects it by uniting the couple spiritually. This spiritual union is considered marriage to God.

Therefore, having sex outside of marriage is so destructive because you are uniting yourself to someone not meant for you nevertheless the spiritual tie and bonding happens. This binding to others outside of marriage creates a soul tie. During sex, the souls are tied together in a spiritual union. When the couple breaks up that binding must be broken the problem is it is not easy to break out of a spiritual binding. A person can remain tied to another person long after a

## SINGLE ONE

breakup for years. This can produce problems in intimacy when a person finally does marry someone.

You must understand this if you want to be free from all your sexual ties you must ask God to break the soul ties you created. Then and only then can you truly belong to the one God intended you to be with! Get free and stay free!

### LET'S TALK ABOUT SEX BABY

As stated before, God created sex from the beginning for the purpose of not just procreation but also for us to enjoy our partner. But when a man and a woman marry, they must also be able to talk openly about what they enjoy in the privacy of their bedroom. Hebrews 13:4 "Marriage should be honored by all and the marriage bed kept undefiled, for God will judge the sexually immoral and adulterers."

A couple must discuss what works for each other.

1) Do we use birth control or not?

## SINGLE ONE

2) Do we use condoms and if so what kind?
3) Some women, like me, are allergic to birth control so it didn't work for me
4) What positions are most comfortable for the woman?
5) What position is most comfortable for the man?
6) If the woman is uncomfortable with a position, then that position is off the table
7) If a man does not want certain things done to him then that is off the table
8) Women crave intimacy like talking, hugging, kissing, fondling
9) Women don't see the actual act of sex itself as intimacy but rather all gestures that lead up to sex. Intercourse itself is the conclusion of fore play for women.
10) Men see the actual act of intercourse as intimacy as a matter of fact men feel loved through the actual act of intercourse. When a wife deprives her husband of sex,

## SINGLE ONE

they feel unloved.

11) Men see fore play like a barrier to having actual sexual intercourse. However, a good man will engage in fore play because he knows his wife needs it

12) Role-play or costumes must be what both people want not just one of you.

13) Be careful with introducing sex toys and other things like these into the bedroom. People may become addicted to outside stimulants and loose interest for their partner over time.

### What about Pornography?

Pornography should never be part of any marriage! Pornography is an industry where women and men are used for the sole purpose of voyeurism. When porn is watched it creates a fake expectation in the relationship where the man or woman feel like they must perform the same acts to get that type of reaction. Pornography brings the idea of using the body

## SINGLE ONE

for evil and creates an atmosphere of immorality. As a couple watches porn, the images become the focus instead of the person they are with. Those images introduce fantasies that do not include your spouse but rather other strangers. For men and women pornography can become an addiction that can take over a person's life. I have heard testimonies from men where their addiction had gotten so bad, they lost their marriages, jobs and friends as they isolated themselves to enjoy their porn. Women can also become addicted to porn and it can lead them to degrade themselves to men as objects and not women. Women have been objectified for years and porn does not make this fact any easier for women. Women live in fear of being raped, molested and kidnapped for the sole purpose of sex.

I know a man who grew up in a home where his father was extremely controlling and overbearing. Since the young man felt completely helpless to change anything to make

## SINGLE ONE

himself feel in control he turned to porn. At first it was magazines. For years this was his secret vice. As he got older his addiction grew and the magazines where not enough. He needed more. When he started working, he began going to strip clubs. Soon the trips to strip clubs were not enough so he graduated to having lap dances by strange women. His wife didn't know this part of his life even existed until she found condoms in their family car one day. She first thought he was cheating on her, so she confronted him with the evidence itself. Well he confessed that he had this addiction and it had grown to lap dances and him lying to his wife about having to work late. His wife was crushed, and she could not believe he had been doing this since he was thirteen. This problem causes the wife great pain. She felt undesired, less then and was afraid of what could happen if her husband's addiction went unchecked. The couple fought for days and there were many tears. The fights became so bad that the wife told her husband I want a divorce because if you cannot see that this behavior is

## SINGLE ONE

disrespectful to me and that you have been unfaithful then there is no point in being together. This marriage almost came to an end. The man became desperate and decided to go into professional counseling. After months of professional counseling, God's intervention, and the man changing his habits completely (no Porn or clubs at all) including him giving his wife a detail account of all his whereabouts the marriage was saved. It took the woman four years to regain the trust she had lost in her husband. This is how destructive porn can be to a couple. It's not worth it. **God created marriage so keep God in your marriage and keep the porn out!**

SINGLE ONE

**Chapter 17**

*Treat Her like a lady*

Why do men treat women like cars in our culture? How many times have you heard a man say "Let's live together first and see if we are compatible?

Men will continue to behave this way because women have accepted the idea that they are cars and men must test drive the vehicle first before

## SINGLE ONE

they purchase it. The problem with this idea is that:

1) women are not objects so they cannot be given the reduced value that is given to an object
2) cars are made by the hands of man so because men are flawed the vehicle maybe defective
3) women are created by a perfect God in the perfect image of God. Every part of you is perfect inside and outside no matter how you see yourself.
4) When men see woman like cars to be tested, what they are really saying is "I don't think your perfect so I have to examine you first and then I will make an evaluation."
5) When a man objectifies a woman when he meets her, he will continue to do the same while in the relationship
6) When men want to objectify a woman what he really wants is a cook, a maid, a laundry mate and a sexual toy
7) God tells us that a woman is "more precious than jewels, rubies and better than gold!"

## SINGLE ONE

8) Men will stop objectifying women when women begin to walk in their rightful place of value
9) Ladies stop giving yourself away for free. Stop trading sex for money or material comforts. If you do this than men will treat you like an object.
10) Men want a woman they can respect and that respects herself as well!
11) Women walk in integrity and faithfulness
12) Take care of yourself

If women want men to respect them then they must begin by respecting themselves. Women who understand their value will not allow men to devalue them or to under mind them as intelligent human beings. Men always want someone to take care of them just like their mom took care of them but it's the way they go about that care that is important.

Recently I was meeting with a woman older than me when God all of sudden gave me some insight into what was going on in the woman's marriage. It was revealed to me that the woman had dimmed her own light to make her husband

## SINGLE ONE

seem to shine brighter. What God told the woman was, God didn't need her help to make her husband look better to others. The reason for this is because if the wife diminishes herself so her husband can shine brighter than is God really with the husband or are you making these concessions to make him look better? Too many women have done this or are doing this right now. Men need our support but dumbing yourself down, refusing to use your gifts because their gifts maybe stronger than your husband is not a solution. As a matter of fact, doing this makes God look weak and unable to cause your husband to grow or shine. God does not need our help to mold or shape a husband or wife become who they truly were sent to earth to be.

When I married my husband, I already had a bachelor's degree and by the time we were married I had obtained a master's degree. I was working as a NYC School teacher and I was making more money than my husband. I never dumbed myself down or made any attempt to

## SINGLE ONE

diminish myself in front of him. I treated him with respect and never threw it up in his face that he didn't have a degree or that I made more money than he did. Respect is not based on credentials, positions or degrees. Respect is given to good men that are loving, honest and hard working. Six months after we were married my husband went back to school and he started from scratch refusing to carry any old credits from his previous schools. He had attended four schools and had dropped out of all of them. He was attending Brooklyn College when I met him, but he only went in when a test was given or a final. Despite all of this he was and is brilliant.

The fact that I did not diminish myself made my husband want to work hard and make something of himself. I never badgered my husband about going to school I merely showed him a good example and reminded him "You don't go to school to make friends with others or to be entertained by your professors. You are confusing school with a long-term residence.

## SINGLE ONE

School is a racetrack. You go around the track pull in to get what you need and when the race is over you move on having gotten what you need from the professor in the pit stops. You go to school to get what you need from them and get out." That one statement worked on my husband's mind and he decided to go back to school with a new sense of purpose and determination.

My husband graduated from NYU's first extended school for adults with the highest honors Summa Cum Lade in 1994. He was then accepted to Harvard University and graduated from there in 1997 with Summa Cum Lade with a degree in law. Today he works for one of the premier law firms in Tampa and is a major partner of the firm. He is the second in command at the firm.

My husband is one of the smartest men I know. He is truly a genius who needed the right guidance and love. A man needs a woman to support his dreams and encourage him to follow

## SINGLE ONE

his dreams. A man needs a woman who believes in him and can see the potential and ability he has. A man doesn't need a woman diminishing herself because then he will become diminish. A man needs a woman who knows when to push, when to encourage and when to stand back.

My life has changed greatly over the course of eighteen years. Not only did God take me out of my job but he prospered my husband so much that even if I were still working at current salary rates my husband would still be making eight times my salary. So, the wonderful man who I originally made more money than, now doesn't need my money at all. God has blessed us so much that my salary is not needed at all. God did all of this because I never diminished myself in my work life, education, or spiritual life. You see I realized early in our relationship through God's wisdom that I did not need to lessen myself but that I had to allow God to use me as a light to his life. As God made me shine my husband followed that light right into his own purpose.

SINGLE ONE

## Chapter 18
### *Treat Him like a Man*

I have learned a great deal from my husband over the course of the last 34 years that we have been together. In this time, he has shared with me some heart felt needs that men have.

Men are very concrete in their thinking and they are not beat around the bush in sharing their dislikes or general feelings about things. The

## SINGLE ONE

insight I will share with you is insight he has shared with me. I also know he does not speak for all men but as a very intelligent extremely well read and aware man, his opinion may shed some light into how to understand men better.

1) Men hear through ears of honor and they filter everything you say through those ears of honor.

2) Women do not emasculate your man by embarrassing him in front of others or talking about your relationship with him to others.

3) Men want a wife, partner in life not a mother! Don't boss them around!

4) If a man senses he is being dishonored, he will react in a negative way and respond according to what he has perceived he has heard.

5) Men require respect. Men can feel disrespected when yelled out or called out of their given name.

## SINGLE ONE

6) Men do not tolerate being belittled or degraded in anyway. Those are fighting statements to them.

7) Men do not like confrontation. Why? Because confrontation leads to physical altercations.

8) Men don't always have to have the last word, but they need to heard.

9) Men need praise more than women do. They want to be acknowledged for any good deeds or work they do.

10) Men need to know you appreciate them.

11) Men need to know you need them not in a needy weak woman way but in a baby, I want and need you in my life.

12) Men want to take care of their wife because it makes them feel capable.

13) Men need to know they are loved.

14) Men need to know you know they are good fathers.

## SINGLE ONE

15) Men need to know that you trust them to take care of the children.

16) Men need a little pride because it helps them move forward in life.

17) Men need to feel accomplished.

18) Men need physical activity almost daily.

19) Men don't mind helping but they don't want to be dumped on.

20) Men hate, hate, hate to be nagged!

21) Men need to come home to clean house that is calm and organized.

22) A man's home is his sanctuary and safe place from the cold world.

23) Men like woman don't want to be criticized or micromanaged.

Not every man is the same but by in large most men would agree with this list I shared with you.

This list is by no means an exhausted list. Women must use wisdom to coexist with their husbands. The bible tells us in the book of

## *SINGLE ONE*

Proverbs "the wise woman with her hands builds up her home, while the foolish one with her hands tears it down!" Don't be a foolish woman!

Try not to turn every other situation into an argument. Learn to not sweat the small stuff. Save your energy for real problems. When real problems come because you have established an atmosphere of respect then you both will be able to manage the stress of any crisis.

My husband and I have observed these simple guidelines in our relationship along with our non-negotiable terms and we have been able to remain together and have become stronger during great loss, death of parents, health issues, loss of jobs, relocating and children about to leave the nest.

## Chapter 19
### *Who Can You Trust?*

Trust means to have faith, charge, believe, and hope or to entrust something to someone. When we trust we are really saying we have belief in a person and what they stand for. When we trust we express a conviction that we have confidence in that person's strength, abilities, and character. When we trust we have

## SINGLE ONE

expectations of the person's behavior and we come to feel confident in relying on them. Trust is giving someone credit for what they can do, bring, develop, create, or manage. Trust is also the ability to develop dependency on a person. The opposite of trust is distrust, unbelief, hopelessness, lack of confidence and non-reliance in the person completely.

The problem with humanity is that the negative attributes they attached to each other they also project them onto God. People convince themselves that God is like human begins and therefore cannot be trusted to manage or guide us in anyway. I am convinced after 19 years of pondering this trust issue that one of the reason people disobey God so easily is because they do not trust Him. But God is not like man at all! God is a spirit and He has been working in man and through man for thousands of years. God is trustworthy, why, because God never lies. God is holy all the time. He is not a man that He should lie nor is He man that requires repentance. God has

## SINGLE ONE

no sin to repent about in the first place. God is perfect. God is what we should aspire to be because He is good, virtuous, kind, patient, generous, loving, forgiving, honest, loyal, thoughtful, peaceful, merciful, and so much more.

We can trust in God for many reasons:
1) God is not man that He should lie
2) God is not like man that must repent himself
3) God is our good Father! The Bible tells us if an earthly father would not give his son a stone when he has asked him for bread, isn't our Heavenly Father better than an earthly father? The answer is yes!

4) Trust means having confidence in the promises of the Lord.
5) T- totally dependent on God
6) R- Righteous God is completely righteous meaning there is no flaw in Him
7) U- Ultimate God has all power
8) S- Shepherd He is our shepherd
9) T-Truth is God and His word is true all the time!

## SINGLE ONE

Examine yourself as to the real reason why you fail to obey God and His word. Could it be that you are categorizing Him as a mere mortal instead of the God He truly is? Remember this, we will be judged by what we know, and what we have ignored as well. We will be judged by all our failures to obey Him and trust in Him. We can lean on God because His desire is for us to trust Him in all things, everything, everyday all the way!

## Chapter 20
### *Go to The Word*

A short while ago I brought a teaching out of Hebrews 4:12,13 "For the word of God is alive and active, sharper than a two edged sword, it penetrates even to dividing the soul and spirit, joints and marrow: it judges the thoughts and attitudes of the heart. Nothing in all creation is hidden from God's sight. Everything is

## SINGLE ONE

uncovered and laid bare before the eyes of Him to whom we must give account."

The word alive means; not dead, alert active, animated, in existence, force or operation. Its synonyms are energetic, vigorous, spry, vital, vivacious, buoyant, exuberant, ebullient, zestful, and spirited.

The word alive in Hebrew is the word chayah (pronounced chi-ya) and it means to have life, remain alive, sustain life, live prosperous, live-forever, be quickened, be alive, and be restored to life or health. It also means to be revived from sickness, discouragement, faintness, and death and to cause to grow.

The word of God has power to make us alive again even if we are dead or dying. God's word can sustain us, keep us or resuscitate us back to life. The word can also restore those areas in our lives that are dead, faint, sick, weary, or disillusioned. God's word is so powerful that it can operate in us and makes us alert, aware, woke, vital again, energetic, and spirited. God's

## SINGLE ONE

word is able to do all of this because it is what God tells us we should be living off. "Man shall not live by bread alone (only) but by every word that proceeds (comes forth or has come forth) out of the mouth of God!" Matthew 4:4

God's word is active! The Greek word for active is energes from which we get the word energy. The word energes means to be engaging or ready in physically energetic pursuits. Its synonymous are; lively, spirited, spry, mobile, vigorous, vital, dynamic and sporty. This word also means; to be effective, productive of due result at work. Which means the word of God will produce something when it is put to or sent to work in a place or person.

Isaiah 55:11 tells us "For the word of God will not return back void but it will produce what it has been sent to do in the thing or place it has been sent to do in." God's word His logos (Jesus is God's demonstrated word in action) (John 1:1) will accomplish what it says it will accomplish everywhere and in everyone it is sent to. God's word produces, gives, sustains, and restores life, health and energizes its host.

You are the host for the word of God and in you and through you God can accomplish great things. When the word of God gets in our heart, mind, spirit and soul, change occurs. You cannot change, be renewed, restored, or resuscitated without the dynamic (dunamas-Greek powerful) explosive word of God.

This is why God's word tells us in Philippians 4:13 "I can do (produce) all things through Christ (the living embodiment of God's spoken creative word) Jesus who strengths (gives life, restores, gives growth) me (the host of God's living word). Paul said in Galatians 2:20, "For now it is not I who lives but Christ who lives in me!"

Get into God's word! Read the word, study it, breathe it in and let it go into your soul, spirit down into the joints and marrow where it will produce new life to live abundantly!

*SINGLE ONE*

## Chapter 21
### *Put family in their proper place*

Luke 14:26 "Jesus said, if anyone come to me and does not hate his own father and mother and wife and children and brothers and sisters, yes and even his own life, he cannot be my disciple."

This verse is highly controversial for some but in accordance with God's word, it is the expectation

## SINGLE ONE

of God for our relationship with God in order that it may function correctly.

There is a biblical Principle in God's word, which on the surface seems simple but many fail to understand it fully and even more fail to practice it. It is the Principle of Priority. The Principle of Priority is found in Exodus 20 where God gives Moses the Ten Commandments. The first commandment is "You will love and serve the Lord your God and Him only will you worship" this is followed by the next command which states "You will not have any other god's before you for the Lord is your God and Him only will you serve." This commandment established that God must be our priority before anything else.

And that no one or anything can come before God in our lives. Our culture has contradicted and continues to oppose this principle by teaching several false hoods:
1) that we must come first before anything or anyone. This has created a culture of selfishness where people have been given cultural

## SINGLE ONE

permission to ignore God as their first focus.

2) This culture then pushed for the family unit to be place above God as well.

3) This also led our culture to assume if "I come first and my family is next then other things can also be placed above and before God

4) so now people place their jobs, their friends, their entertainment above God as well

5) God is being systematically erased from people's life's which is obviously a master plan of lies from the devil

6) removing God from our life's as a priority gives the devil the opportunity to distance man more and more away from a relationship with God

**Psalms 37:4,5** "Delight yourself in the Lord and He will give you the desires of your heart. Commit yourself to the Lord: and He will do this." This Psalm clearly states that we are to delight in God first and then He will give us what our heart desires.

## SINGLE ONE

We can run after what we desire first and then think God will support that when we have failed to delight, serve, honor, respect Him first!

In Revelations chapter 2,3 and 4 the Lord Jesus gives a stern punishment and consequence to one of the 7 churches He addresses. "I have a charge against you (the church) that you have abandoned your first love. For this my God in heaven will not recognize you when you stand before Him." In other words if we leave our first love which should be God and follow after other loves first, (husband, wife, family, job, and everything else) then we will be rejected by God as we have rejected Him here on earth.

When we put God first in our life's He blesses us, and He blesses the other relationships in our lives as well. God is a God of relationship who seeks out a monogamous relationship (you and God first). When we place others above Him, we are considered adulterers in the sight of God. Put God first and be blessed!

## Chapter 22
### *Get Rid of the Filth*

**James 1:12** "Therefore get rid of all moral filth and evil that is so prevalent and humbly accept the word planted in you, which can save you!"

The word of God must be planted in you in order for it to take root and become anchored in you. It is only once the word is anchored that it becomes resistant to anything or anyone removing it from you. When the word of God is anchored it is weighted in our hearts to bring about much needed spiritual, moral, emotional, and mental changes.

The implanted word cannot abide in a heart, mind or spirit that is still infected by sin and immoral behavior. Immoral and evil behavior infects, rots, destroys and eventually displaces the seed of the word of God to the point where the seed dies even before it can be birthed or produce fruit.

We cannot allow others to try to destroy the seed of God's word. People can pour doubt and fear on your seed. They can tell you this dream or plan of God for your life seems way too big to achieve. How will you do all of this? Will it cut into your freedom? Will it interfere with your job, family, friends, and others? What will you get from all of this? These are just some of the poisonousness words that people will try to pour over your seed. Words of doubt are also whispered into our ears by the devil himself. Remember the devil is

## SINGLE ONE

not your friend. If he was able to get Adam and Eve kicked out of heaven, fall into disobedience, and become separated from God then what do you think his words can do to you if you are not anchored in God's Word! Remember Satan also injected himself into Cain's thoughts and convinced him that God had rejected his offering and love his brother Able more. That one thought led Cain to kill his own brother!

Beware of family as well. Just because someone is related to you does not mean they want what God wants for you. Too often in families there is a real jealousy especially if they can see a notable change in your courage, self-esteem, and spiritual usefulness in the Lord. Families can at times also try to persuade their loved ones that they are not being directed by God and that they need to live more practical and less spiritual life's. They may even speak evil of your leaders or try to convince you that your leaders are off base, not led by God or are missing some obvious

### SINGLE ONE

spiritual happenings. Therefore, we must make sure the Lord is leading us.

The word of God needs your prayer, your faithfulness, your knowledge of the word and it needs you to maintain and sustain an empowered relationship with God. The Holy Spirit fueled by God's presence and guided by our Lord Jesus waters the word of God.

## Chapter 23
### *Sexual Discrimination*

The Bible tells us that "there is no partiality with God," this simply means God is impartial and sees us all the same, as His children. Yet growing up in the church I saw and experienced sexual discrimination. Some denominations have gone so far as to not allowing women to teach men in the church because of one verse. The verse quoted is by Paul

## SINGLE ONE

where he states, "the woman will be silent in the congregation and not teach the men." I am paraphrasing. I Corinthians 14:34

The issue with this verse is that it was written to one church only meaning it was specific to that one congregation. Secondly the women in that church had founded the church because they were wealthy, and their husbands were not. These wealthy women founded the construction of the church. This church was made up of women and men who had come out of a religious cult where women were in charge and men were subservient to them. Women served a female goddess named Diana. Once a year, women of this cult would chase the men through the streets and capture them as a prize. These women received the Lord into their hearts and were now trying to live out the gospel. Paul had to address the women in this church for several reasons:

1) the women held all the wealth
2) the women founded and built the church

## SINGLE ONE

3) the women supported the church financially

4) the women were using their power to dictate what was happening in the church

5) the women were not letting the men speak or hold positions of power within the church

Paul had to address this because based on the teaching of Jesus "we are all one body in Christ." Paul had to correct their behavior, but nowhere did Paul say women were never to speak or teach at all. Paul was telling the women to give the men a chance. Paul was not anti-women. How do I know this because:

1) Paul's Ministry was largely supported by women

2) Paul had women serving in his ministry as fellow ministers

3) Paul had women smuggle the word from town to town because they were never searched

4) Paul repeatedly thanked women for their love and help in his ministry in the closing of his letters

5) Paul anointed his first Elder Juno a woman and called her "the most worthy apostle of

## SINGLE ONE

Christ" (Priscilla, Joanna, Chloe, Mary, Tryphena, Persis, Julia, the mother of Rufus, Euodia, Syntyche, Nympha, Apphia, Claudia, Lydia, Dorcus, Mary Magdalene) This list is just a small list of the woman that are mentioned. There may have been others that were never mentioned at all.

I, at an early age, did not believe in women as Pastors because it was drilled into my head by my dad. My mom however always pointed out that the men Pastor were the ones falling into sin while no woman Pastor had ever fallen into sin. If God truly is not a respecter of persons, we are either going to practice that in our churches or not.

I am here to tell you all, that God calls those He chooses and anoints them to do His Kingdom work. Never allow any church, denomination, church council or any church leader tell you what your place in God is. God not man dictates your position in God. If your current church experience is telling you that as a woman you can't be a minister in your church, then find

**SINGLE ONE**

another church that believes God can use anyone and He does not discriminate!

SINGLE ONE

## Chapter 24
### *It's Time to Tell your Secret*

It's no secret that children both boys and girls are sexually abused and molested in this country. Too often people who have been abused carry around this secret for years never telling anyone not even their parent. Many abusers are usually a stepparent, relative, boyfriend, uncle, cousin or even a sibling. Abusers usually groom the child for months before abusing the child. As

## SINGLE ONE

the monster grooms the child, they gain their trust first, shower them with gifts, activities, or attention to the point that the child comes to trust the monsters. Another way they groom the child is to convince the child that their home life is sacred, and they cannot talk about their home life to anyone. The monsters will stress the idea of "we are family, and no one can understand our family better than we can." These monsters thrive on isolating and cutting off their victims from all possible help from anyone. Such adults are called Pedophiles. A pedophile is s person who develops a sexual attraction to a child and convinces himself or herself that engaging in a sexual act with a child is not wrong because they are merely loving them. This behavior in our culture is not new. There is evidence that during the time of Caligula and the Roman Empire men took boys as lovers. The thought is completely disgusting and demented. But these monsters still exist in our society today.

## SINGLE ONE

Technology has increased the opportunities for abusers to find their victims. They use chat rooms, take over private cameras by hacking into them and pretend to be children online to begin conversations with children. Still other abusers choose their victims through relationships with insecure lonely men and women who are so desperate to have someone in their life's that they ignore clear signs that a new boyfriend or girlfriend has a pattern of being very interested only in people with children.

Children are not equipped to protect themselves. Parents must be vigilant and protect their children from all outsiders and insiders as well. Children should never be left alone in a home with a boyfriend or girlfriend. A parent must always know whom they are exposing their children to. Children must be taught to tell, tell, and tell, about any behavior from a person that makes them feel uncomfortable. Children must be taught that their bodies belong to them and no one has the right to touch, rub, or uncover

## SINGLE ONE

their private parts ever. Children must be taught to yell, scream, punch, and bite and draw attention to themselves if they feel they are in trouble. Children must be taught to tell their teachers who are trained to handle all cases of suspected child abuse immediately. All educators, doctors, childcare workers, counselors, lawyers, law enforcement personnel and ministers are mandated reporters of all abuse. Parents must train their children to come to them with any concerns or weird behavior anyone has demonstrated towards them. Monsters don't wear mask or disguises! Monsters can be a relative, a neighbor and a stranger.

As a former educator and Principal, I dealt with many abuse cases. Many of those cases involved a stepfather or an uncle of some kind. I have had men arrested right out of their jobs, homes and have participated in sting operations where I had to protect the victims and hide them from their abusers. It broke my heart every time, made me

## SINGLE ONE

angry and caused many sleepless nights for me. But in every instance, there was one constant, a disengaged parent who either didn't care, was too busy, had no or little regard for their children or where their happiness mattered more to them than their children's well- being. In every case the children were left unprotected and ended up suffering in the hands of their perpetrator.

How do so many abusers get away with this behavior? As stated before, abusers groom their victims first. They create an environment of secrecy to isolate their actions. Once the abuser begins the behavior, he or she will threaten the child with bodily harm. But it does not stop there. They also threaten everyone the child loves. Doing this makes their victims become more submissive and compliant with the abuse. When these children finally get away from their abusers great damaged has been deeply imbedded.

Abusers thrive in their harming of children through intimidation, fear, and secrecy. Adults

## SINGLE ONE

who have been abused can only achieve healing from abuse by telling their story repeatedly. Here are some detailed actions that can help abused victims regain their power and heal from their abuse.

1) Take immediate legal action. Most states have now extended their statues of limitations for reporting abuse.

2) Get yourself into treatment. You cannot walk through this type of trauma without professional help. (A psychiatrist, or Psychologist can help)

3) Get spiritual help as well through a church. Lay ministers are also equipped to help people through these situations.

4) It was not your fault! You did nothing to bring this behavior on yourself.

5) I know many cultures do not believe in therapy but going around angry, bitter, drunk, or ending up in a mental institution is worst.

## SINGLE ONE

6) Abusers thrive on secrecy so blow their world apart, by telling what they have done. Don't ever protect an abuser because doing that makes it possible for them to hurt other children.

7) Join a support grow where you can talk to others who completely understand what you have been through.

8) Learn self-defense. I find abused victims become very empowered when they know they can protect themselves.

9) Talk about it all the time. Every time you share your truth you are released from a little more of the pain and damage that was done to you.

10) Remind yourself that you are a survivor and therefore you are a victor not a victim.

11) Abuse is of any kind is criminal and cannot be tolerated by anyone under any circumstance. You deserve to live a life of

## SINGLE ONE

freedom, peace, and joy. God created you to be His child and to be free of all harm. Walk in your truth today! Tell your secret!

# Chapter 25
## *Communication*

Everyone speaks about communication but do we really know what that means. Communication involves much more than just talking.

Communication from the word communicates. To communicate is to express one's thoughts, ideas, opinions, observations, evaluations, objections and concerns about a variety of topics. To be able to communicate with another human being means to share observations, insights, and motivating thoughts. To communicate does not mean to agree with everything someone tells you. To communicate does not mean to be disagreeable because your view is not being received. To communicate does not mean to inject what you think the person is thinking or feeling because you are not in that person's head or heart no matter how long you have known them. To communicate does not mean to put words in a person's mouth either. To expect for someone to always agree or always see things your way is a clear sign you are too immature to have an adult conversation.

Too often people think that when someone disagrees with them it means they are being misunderstood, dismissed, or ignored. If someone disagrees it is a clear sign that they are hearing you. Communication involves listening more and speaking less. If we truly are listening,

## SINGLE ONE

we should be able to restate what the person has said to you.

By the way, a disagreeing opinion is not the end of the world either. All excellent relationships have mastered the skill of communicating effectively with their partner whether to share info, plan an event, or resolve a conflict! If you cannot communicate with at least one person in your life, then you will not be able to communicate with your husband or wife.

Here are some guidelines that will help you become a better communicator.

1) Listen to understand not undermine
2) Listen to understand not solve any problem
3) Problem solving conversations require a different pattern of conversation
4) Listen without interrupting. Interrupting causes you to stop listening.
5) Repeating what someone has said to you will help you demonstrate you are

## SINGLE ONE

listening. You can use this statement "I hear you saying" then add what you heard the person say.

6) The listener can let you know if the statement repeated was correct

7) Eye contact must be maintained

8) Voices must not be raised

9) No mind reading! Mind reading is making statement like "I know you feel this way or I know you are upset or I know you do not want or like my friends, I know you think this or that". You cannot read any one's mind.

10) Be polite as you listen and respond. This shows respect toward others

The application of these communication skills will help improve conversations and make your time more fruitful.

SINGLE ONE

## Chapter 26
### *Your Work is not in vain*

I want to encourage you today that nothing you do for the Lord, the Kingdom of God or others will ever be in vain.

"The Bible tells us do not become weary in well doing for in due time you will reap what you have sown."

That word weary means: tired, exhausted,

## SINGLE ONE

fatigued, worn out, burned out or beaten down. But it also means not to become discouraged, disillusioned, not to let up or become disengaged, disconnected, or despondent in anyway.

That word due means: appointed time, in its season, in its appropriate time, in its time of completeness, its time of fullness, in its rightful timely moment and perfected season.

We cannot let go of doing well for God or others. God promises to make sure the good we do is accounted to us, credited to us. It's like having a spiritual debt card that when you need something from God your account will be in good standing with God and a withdrawal can be made on your behalf.

We don't do things for God or others to get something in return but it's good to know that the Lord is a "rewarder" of those who faithfully serve Him.

**SINGLE ONE**

So, hang on! Be faithful to God in all things and He will be faithful to bless you when you need it most!

**SINGLE ONE**

## Chapter 27
### *What's My Worth?*

Who or what determines your worth? Too many women and men place their own self-worth on how people perceive them rather than on moral and dignity filled character traits. You do not have to be rich or famous to feel self-worth. God created us to be human beings capable of great acts of bravery, love, mercy, and selfless action. Sometimes however people are

## SINGLE ONE

subjected to trauma where they become diminished in their own minds simply because someone deemed them less then or powerless or their power was taken from them as children.

From birth to five years of age a child's character, moral behavior, likes, and dislikes are being form. This is also the time when a child's psychological personality is also forming. This means that during this very critical stage of crucial development a child's mind can be destroyed or built up depending on what is poured into that child. A child that is taught that materials things determine their worth will grow up with an unsatisfied need to have things all the time in order to feel happy. The problem with this is that the happy feeling a person gets from a recent purchase doesn't last. The feeling wears off and in order to get it back the person must once again buy something else or more to produce the same high they felt before. The same is true for children who are taught not to share and guard everything they have, grow up to be

## SINGLE ONE

people who literally struggle with sharing things or even space with others. I grew up pretty poor. In 1979 when I applied for college, my family's income was $20,000 and we were a family of six at the time. As a result of a very limited income my family struggled financially quite often. I am one of three sisters and each of us has at least one hoarding behavior. My hoarding behavior is clothing, shoes, and bags. Why, because as a child I remember having two pairs of shoes. One for school one for church. In Junior High School I had to wear sneakers to gym class, so I owned my first pair of sneakers in Jr. High School. My older sister hoards pants and shoes. My little sister hoards lotions, hand creams and medicine. I never notice this until my little sister bought her first house and I walked into her bathroom and I saw all the lotions. I couldn't believe how much she had. That's when it hit me that we all had carried into adulthood the fear of not having enough of something. So, when we do shop, we over do those items we longed for and never had enough of as children. I have become so aware of

## SINGLE ONE

this now that I started 19 years ago to go through my closet and give away or donate at least a 1/3 of what I own every year.

This one act has given me a sense of security and renewed trust in God that if I need something, He will provide it for me, and I don't have to hoard anything. This revelation came to me when my walk-in closet collapsed days before I had to teach at a major conference over the course of a whole weekend. I was so angry and asked God why this happening to me and why now? He answered me very clearly in an audible voice, "You have too much. Give it to others who need it." Since then I have been clothing woman going back to the work force, those who need different articles of clothing or just because. It is my way of acknowledging to God that my value is not found in the things I own but in the security that He has me and is my provider.

Where does your value lie? What are you hoarding out of fear and insecurity?

## SINGLE ONE

The Bible tells us our value is found in God. Proverbs 31 tells us beauty fades but a woman who serves the Lord will be praised.

People want to be noticed or praised for what they wear, how their hair is styled or what type of shoes they wear. However, at the end of every life no one ever regrets not having the right clothes, shoes or hair. People do regret not having loved more sincerely, not doing more for others and not loving the Lord with

more passion. They regret not giving God more time and devotion. The only problem is that at the end of our life there will be no more time to get it right. There will be no more time to focus on what you do have rather than on what you don't have.

The Bible tells us "don't be desperate to store up treasure on earth where decay, mold and worms can destroy it all but rather store up treasure in heaven where it will never decay." Matthew 16:20, 21

**SINGLE ONE**

What are you focused on? Does your clothes, hair, shoes, and bags matter more to you than your soul? Psalm 37 "Delight yourself in the Lord and He will give you the desires of your heart." Are you delighting yourself in God or in your material desires? It is time to switch your focus from the material to the spiritual!

## Chapter 28
### *Where is your Love?*

There are times when people will question your love and the expression of that love. However, the same people who question your heart felt motives do so because of a few reasons:

1) They are not receiving that from anyone, so they are insecure of those who show love

**SINGLE ONE**

2) They are jealous of the progress they see happening to people who are loved

3) They haven't taken the time to get to know the person who is helping and acting out of kindness

4) They don't understand how God's love works nor are they able to express it

5) The Bible tells us "if you have not love you have not God because God is love"

6) They can see people hurting but do nothing about it

7) They are insecure about people loving them because someone mistreated them that should have love them

8) Real love is self-sacrificing

If you have a friend, mentor or someone who truly cares about your spiritual growth and is showing you how real love is demonstrated, keep them close. Let God use them in your life to help you obtain God's purpose for your life.

## Chapter 29
### *Who are you listening to?*

We cannot give the devil an inch because he will take a yard. How do we give the enemy an inch in our lives? We do this by entertaining or paying attention to the thoughts he whispers in our ears.

The Bible tells us that "God must take our thoughts captive" II Corinthians 10:5 why?

## SINGLE ONE

Because God knows that if we give the enemies whispers too much attention, he will take those thoughts and run with them. All the devil does is introduce a thought, but we take that thought and build on it.

I know this firsthand because this is how the enemy tries to get to me. He whispers a negative thought about anything or anyone and if I add to that thought the next thing I know, I am upset and angry. Then I begin to feel unappreciated, unloved, and hopeless. Then I begin to blame God for allowing all these people to hurt me and lastly, I say to myself why bother to do anything for God at all. By this point I am sad, depressed and feeling completely defeated.

Don't give the devil a platform for your thoughts. I have found that when the devil whispers a negative thought into my ear and I counteract that thought with the word of God, the thoughts stop. Sometimes I have to speak out loud to the enemy and tell him "you're a liar devil, God said I am victorious." When I remind the devil of what

## SINGLE ONE

God has said about me the enemy leaves me alone.

The devil only wants to point out what's wrong with you, your failings and the failings of others. He wants you to continue to be angry with the people who hurt you. He wants you to be unforgiving. He wants you to remain bitter forever. If he can accomplish this, then he has done his job. He has managed to destroy God's plan for your life. He has managed to kill you spiritually as well.

Don't let the devil take your mind or life over. Fight back! Call on the Lord. The mind cannot think Godly thoughts and entertain the enemy's thoughts at the same time. You must fight fire with Fire! God's word is a sword of Fire use it!!

We must stay spiritually alert before God. Paul teaches in Romans 13:11-14

"Besides this, knowing the time, it is already the hour for you to wake up from sleep, for now our salvation is nearer than when we first believed. The night is nearly over, and the daylight is near,

## SINGLE ONE

so let us discard the deeds of darkness and put on the armor of light. Let us walk with decency, as in the daylight: not in carousing and drunkenness, not in sexual impurity and promiscuity; not in quarreling and jealousy. But put on the Lord Jesus Christ, and make no plans to satisfy the fleshly desires."

This is the word of the Lord. Walk in daylight or walk in the light of the salvation of the Lord because night is almost over. This night is referring to the darkness of sin and Satan's reign over the world. We cannot live a double life. We cannot live for the Lord and still practice actions of darkness. It's time to wake up put on the armor of light and walk into the light and stay in the light!

*SINGLE ONE*

## Chapter 30
## *Why Can't I move forward from this?*

Do you know people that just can't move forward after a relationship? There are many reasons for this:
1) The person has formed a soul tie (a soul tie is a spiritual bond that forms when two people have sex. Like a ventral disease it hangs on to you) or there's a friendship of jealousy

## SINGLE ONE

2) The person has convinced himself or herself that they cannot do better than their former partner
3) They want to be in a relationship even if it is toxic
4) They are settling for a lesser person
5) The former partner has damaged you emotionally and psychologically
6) Your trying to find your child a daddy or mommy (kids need mentally healthy parents not nut jobs fly by people)
7) The person has over romanticized marriage
8) Marriage is very hard and requires two completely invested people
9) You are a child of divorce or abandonment, so you want to have a Brady Bunch family
10) You think a person in your life makes you more legit to others (not so by the way)

If you don't have patience for foolishness, if you don't like people in your space all the time, if you can't see yourself with one person for a lifetime, then forget marriage. Marriage takes all your patience, unselfishness, sacrifice, forgiveness,

## SINGLE ONE

mercy, compassion, and the ability to let small things go! If you believe you have a soul tie seek out deliverance from a reputable ministry who have been trained to help people receive deliverance.

Being set free from a soul tie requires commitment to staying free. The first step is to be delivered the next step is to rid yourself of everything that person has ever given you, pictures, and jewelry. Spirits attach themselves to objects and use them to keep you gripped to a person. Some people add spells to objects so they can keep tabs on your whereabouts.

I recently met with a young married woman and we were talking about ministry, her children and some things that had happened in her past in ministry. She spoke of a friend that no matter how much time had gone by she always seem to know when to call her when trouble was brewing for her or when she was about to make a major move in her life and family. The minute she shared that I heard the Lord tell me, "She has a piece of jewelry and that is how she is keep an

## SINGLE ONE

account on her life." I interrupted the woman and asked her if her friend had ever given her a piece of jewelry, she said yes how did I know? I immediately told her she had to find that necklace and get rid of it because she had attached a visual window spell to that necklace, so she was able to see into her life. I told her do not touch the necklace with your bare hands use plastic gloves and throw it away far from your house. Why the gloves? The gloves are necessary so that no further physical contact takes place. I am happy to report that the woman went home looked through her jewelry and found the necklace and threw it out. The woman has not been able to contact her, nor has she found out any other moves the woman has made with her husband or family.

## Chapter 31
### *What are you planting in your life?*

The Bible tells us that our choices will lead to a portion of production, but what you produce will reflect whatever you plant.

Galatians 6:7 "Be not deceived God will not be mocked, whatever a man sows that will he also reap".

This scripture clearly tells us that God will judge

## SINGLE ONE

us by what we plant. If we plant seeds of hate, unforgiveness, jealousy, adultery, fornication, lying, lust, evil, hurt, abuse, disobedience, theft, blasphemy, drunkenness, witchcraft and idolatry we will gather a harvest that represents the seeds we planted. After all you cannot plant onion seeds and expect to get sweet apples from your tree.

Galatians 5 also tells us to walk in the Spirit and produce fruit of the spirit. These fruits are love, peace, joy, patience, hope, kindness, forgiveness, humbleness, and

generosity. These nine attributes if planted will produce good fruit for you and others.

Those who plant the seeds of the flesh (jealousy, hatred, malice, pride, lust, fighting, strive, witchcraft, immorality, anger, idolatry, drunkenness, strive, contention, selfishness, vanity, pride, murmuring, and blasphemy) will have the fruit of the flesh come back to them. These sinful seeds produced by people who do not serve God or who are playing church (you go

## SINGLE ONE

to church maybe on Sundays but Monday through Saturday you live however and you are doing whatever your flesh desires) think they are getting away with something. They believe that the Bible is for everyone else not them. They also believe they can justify their behavior by telling God "I am young, and you only live once". **Though yes, we only live once we also will die only once.** God has given us all one chance at life to get it right with God, others, and ourselves.

Our production of good fruit (kindness, mercy, forgiveness, love) also helps others by seeing a real God expressed through your life and in your actions. Our good actions are obvious evidence that something good is in your heart. Without real evidence of true goodness then what are you truly putting out of your heart? The Bible tells us "it is counted to a man to die once and after this death and judgment will come." Hebrews 9:27

What will you have to show God? What fruit have you produced during a lifetime of planting? What are you planting in yourself and others? Has your

## SINGLE ONE

fruit blessed anyone else on earth while you were alive? Has anyone grown as a result of your testimony? We are individuals but God has called us to behave and treat others like a community. God is a God of community building between Himself, His children and between His children and each other.

Take thought of your life this year. The definition of insanity is doing the same thing repeatedly and expecting to get a different result!!!!

Blessings

SINGLE ONE

## Chapter 32
### *What's the difference between a boyfriend and a husband?*

A boyfriend is interested in having a good time. He wants to share his time with someone. A husband is looking to share his lifetime with someone with whom he can build a life. Don't be boyfriend material be husband material. Don't be girlfriend material be wife material.

## SINGLE ONE

material. Don't be girlfriend material be wife material.

As the holidays begin to approach, I know some of my single ladies and gents are putting in their request for a spouse. God made Adam and gave him Eve because "it wasn't good for man to be alone." But do you know what qualities a man or woman should have? Have you made your list specific to God as to what a mate should be like? I am not talking about tall dark and handsome. That is superficial. The Bible tells us beauty fades over time. What then?

What character traits should my mate have?

1) A relationship with God

2) honesty

3) understanding

3) truthful

4) loving and affectionate with me and my family

5) hard working with healthy ambition

6) kind

7) thoughtful

8) able to appreciate your gifts and talents

## SINGLE ONE

without jealousy

9) family centered

10) humor

11) forgiving

12) generous

These traits are very close to the character traits that God Himself demonstrates towards His children.

I asked God to give me a man who was loving, kind, affectionate, understanding and who could appreciate my gifts and talents. These are the only qualities I asked God for in a mate, but God in His wisdom gave me everything on this list plus more. He gave me a man who is super intelligent and compassionate. God saw into my future and He added to my list. God gave me a real man who protects, loves, and nurtures his children, a real leader. A man I learned to trust with my heart.

I know I could not have come this far in my life, ministry, or relationships without him. God your Father wants to give you the best, don't undercut

## SINGLE ONE

yourself by settling for less. You cannot turn a sow's ear into a silk purse!

What does this mean? It means you my dear do not have the power to change any man or woman no matter what you do. Too many women run themselves into the ground and live secret miserable lives. They pretend they are happy, but they are not. Their husbands or wife lies, manipulates their feelings, and convince them they are wrong when they are right. They are poor examples to their children and their children end up not respecting either of their parents. Actually no one respects them or believes their words. Respect yourself enough to walk away. Don't let your pride keep you trapped!

## Chapter 33
### *What are men really thinking?*

My husband shared with me the inner thoughts of how men really think.

1) Men are concrete thinkers. They truly say what they mean. When a man says, "I don't want children" they mean it.

2) Men begin to withhold the truth from you when they see that the truth gets a woman upset

## SINGLE ONE

and causes her to get emotional. When a woman becomes emotional it teaches a man that he cannot be completely honest with her.

3) I had to learn to stop overreacting or getting too emotional so that my husband could feel comfortable telling me the truth.

4) Men cannot handle overly emotional reactions. I hope this helps some of you to communicate more effectively with men.

**Single Ladies**: My husband has shared with me a ton of secrets men will never tell women about. When a man meets his mate, he will waste no time to put a ring on it and close the deal. Men know immediately if you are the one. Men are primitive in their approach to mating with someone. A man can be with someone to "fill up the time" for years but not marry her. When he meets the one, he will drop the "fill up girl" and marries the one in three months tops! Truth: Don't be the fill up time girl. Walk away if he's not moving towards a permanent relationship with you in a matter of 6-8 months!

SINGLE ONE

## Chapter 34
### *Loose the nasty girl!*

Have you ever asked yourself why you have a bad attitude, a short temper or can be so unpleasant with others? No child is born with a bad attitude but rather they learn how to interact and communicate with others from what they observed their parents do in front of them.

A child that watches their parent's lie to other will learn that lying is acceptable and needed to be able to deal with others. Lying will also lead children to behave dishonestly. Children who observe their parents use spending money as a way to make themselves feel better, will learn to use shopping as a way to cope with bad feelings instead of confronting those feelings, working through it and growing from it. A child that is taught to keep secrets will grow up to be secretive and dishonest with their partner. Children who are not taught how to handle crisis without losing their heads will find it difficult to cope with crisis in their lives.

My mom was a very emotional woman. She could not handle crisis involving her own children or husband. She was great at handling financial crisis because her grandfather who raised her was a businessman. My mom knew how to manage money, save it and balance it in our home. But if anyone in the family had an accident, this strong financial woman would buckle over scream and become completely useless to her kids and husband. For example,

## SINGLE ONE

my dad was working under his nephews Volkswagen van and all of a sudden, the jack popped, and my dad tried to get out from under the van. However, his hand did not make it completely out. My dad ran into the house with his hand bleeding. My mom and older sister started screaming and running around like chickens without heads. Meanwhile my dad was bleeding. I had to step in and took my dad's hand into the bathroom sink and I yelled out to my mom to stop screaming and get me the dishwashing liquid. I told my dad this is going to hurt a lot brace yourself dad. My dad's hand was covered in grease. I had to wash and scrub all the grease off so I could see what was left of his finger. My dad's thumb was split in half and I could see the bone. At this point I knew I had to clean all the dirt and grease out, so I could take him to the emergency room. I told my dad he needed stiches. At one point I wanted to study medicine because I am not squeamish around blood, guts or wounds. When my cousin and I took my dad to the emergency room they

## SINGLE ONE

immediately took him into a room. When the doctor saw my dad's hand wrapped up in a towel, I could see him brace himself for what that hand would look like. When the doctor at Kings County Hospital in Brooklyn removed the towel, my dad was missing his nail bed and the thumb was opened completely up the middle down to the wrist. The doctor's first question was what happened followed by who cleaned your hand? My dad told him I had scrubbed his hand with dishwashing liquid. The doctor told me you did an amazing job and probably saved his hand from infection and you sterilized it at the same time. The doctor asked if I was considering going to medical school. I told him I had considered it, but I was going into education. My dad received nine stitches on the inside to put together the exploded finger back to the shape of a finger and he received ten stiches on the outside of his finger as well. My dad never suffered any infection or had any loss of feeling in his thumb. My dad told me days later in front of my mom.

## SINGLE ONE

If Lydia had not jumped in and kept her cool, I would have lost my thumb.

For a person to change, they have to identify the bad or useless behavior and let go of the bad attitude. The following steps will help you.

1) Think before you speak, you are not a mannequin with a person's hand in your back!
2) Control your emotions. No one cares for your gross mouth.
3) Teach yourself how to stay cool under pressure because life is not going to be easy everyday
4) If you want respect you have to prove you are worthy of that respect.
5) People respect people who respect themselves first.
6) Attitude has nothing to do with a person's surroundings it has to do with how you see yourself
7) A good attitude opens doors but a bad one will close those same doors
8) Can God change your attitude? Yes, He can but

## SINGLE ONE

you need to cooperate with the change.

9) It takes less energy to be kind then it does to be rude, obnoxious, bickering, trifling, and annoying. Only no one thinks it's cute.

10) Your real friends will tell you about yourself! Be real don't be crude!

11) Practice counting down before exploding and remember you don't have to share every silly, negative or opinion with everyone

12) Practice the pulse. Pulse before you speak, pulse before you add your two cents

13) Finally no amount of justification goes unnoticed! Admit your failings and change your behavior!!!

Change in behavior is hard but good behavior practices make us better people.

SINGLE ONE

## Chapter 35
### *Do you know what you want?*

Single people often lament not having a relationship and they think that being with a person will change or cure all of their problems. I thought that too. But marriage allows us to not be alone even though some very married people still experience loneness. What marriage does is

## SINGLE ONE

it opens areas in our lives that we have never thought to discuss or ponder.

Every single person should conduct a personal inventory of himself or herself before they enter a lifelong commitment with someone. Some questions that you may want to ask yourself are the following:

1) Am I the kind of person who likes to be surrounded by others?
2) Am I a person who enjoys being alone?
3) Am I easily irritated by things like people chewing with their mouths open, messy people, a toilet seat left up, doing dirty laundry, folding it, cooking for others?
4) Am I a person who needs to be right all the time?
5) Am I an argumentative person?
6) Am I moody?
7) Do I have unresolved sexual issues?

## SINGLE ONE

8) Do I have unresolved eating disorders, mental health issues or issues of insecurity?

You must know what you truly want from a relationship. Some questions you should be asking yourself:

1) Do I want to be married because that is what my family, friends or society expects?

2) Do I enjoy being in a relationship with someone but I really don't want a lifelong commitment?

3) Do I want children? Does he want children?

4) I don't want children, but I do want to be married. Is there something wrong with me?

5) Is it wrong to want children but not want to be married?

6) Should I tell him I don't want children?

7) Can I adopt and be a single mom?

8) I want children, but he doesn't. Do I stay and pray he changes his mind over time?

You cannot wait until you are in a committed relationship to decide the answers to these

## SINGLE ONE

questions. You must know yourself. Keep in mind in some cases (very few) people grow and change over time but you still need to have a general idea of what you want for yourself.

When I was nine years old a private lesson music teacher touched me in an inappropriate way. I was confused about the whole thing and I felt feelings I had never felt before. My dad and other parents ran him out of town. This event happened in my mother's house in her living room. This one event created a horrible block and dirty feelings about sex. These feelings persisted into my marriage and caused problems for me. It was horrible because I loved my husband, but I had a hard time feeling comfortable with him. I thank God for His intervention in my life. With his help I was able to deal with what happened to me. I was also able to confront my parents about how they never got me the help I needed. They thought by having me suppress my memories that would be enough. When I confronted my parents,

*SINGLE ONE*

they were able to apologize to me for their failures. I needed to be free, so I had to take control over what had happened to me.

Sexual Harassment, molestation or rape of any kind is deeply evil!

A man who does these things to children or women of any age are led by the devil himself to destroy that females esteem and to kill all trust she may have. This evil is also about stripping the woman of power. By demeaning a woman in this way, they diminish her as well. Too many of us have remained quiet for years. Who are we protecting? We are not really protecting our selves we are protecting the perpetrator. Stop protecting the devil and his agents. Speak up, tell someone, shout it from the rooftop. In doing so it will liberate you as it liberated me!

Be free because God wants you to be free!

# Chapter 36
## *RED FLAGS*

Red flags are used in traffic stops, construction sites and aviation to warn those around of possible danger or pit falls. Too many people ignore the "early warning signs" at the beginning of a relationship. The problems you ignore in the beginning will be problems that you ignore in the beginning will be the problems that will eventually tank you relationship later.

## SINGLE ONE

If she or He does the following, consider these red flags:

1) They seem very interested in anything that benefits them but not as interested in your goals, ideas, or interest.
2) They are dismissive of the things that worry or concern you
3) They make you feel guilty if you do not call them or text hem all the time
4) They like to flirt even in front of you (calls, cheating)
5) They like to look at other men or women
6) They are very secretive about their past (they use drugs, alcohol)
7) They are obsessed about having material things
8) They want to move up in the world, but they don't have a plan nor are they interested in making it happen
9) They be little you or insult you
10) They are violent when angry
11) They make a small argument a big deal

## SINGLE ONE

12) They are very jealous
13) They want to spend time around their family but not yours
14) They criticize you in a joking manner

This is but a short list however I have seen women and men ignore these and then end up in a very unhappy marriage.

I have spoken to many men/women who have come out of bad relationships and when I ask them "Did you see any signs when you first started dating?" After they beat around the bush for a little while they finally answer the question the same way. Yes I saw these things, but I thought after we were married, he/she would change. This is the same old story of "when I marry him/her/ my love will change him/her. My reaction and response are always the same, and you still married him/her.

I have a cousin who is about 87 years old now but when she was in her twenties, she married a young man who was very attentive and jealous over her. She thought it was love. Once they were

## SINGLE ONE

married and the kids came, he changed. He began isolating her from family and friends. He would beat her for any reason including her attendance at church. After twenty-three years she had had enough. She planned her escape and one of her sons helped hide her in Puerto Rico. He searched everywhere for her. He even called my mom to ask her if she knew where she was, but my mom didn't know. My mom even told him if I did know I wouldn't tell you. My cousin has suffered for years, was hospitalized for broken bones and all for love! That is not love! All the signs were there from the beginning of her relationship, but she ignored them and thought she could make him better. We cannot change anyone ever! People who truly love you can try hard to adjust, but major character changes are very hard for people. Only with God's help and extreme self-reflection and psychological help can people adjust themselves.

Don't ignore the red flags or signs in your relationship! Infidelity, lying, flirting, keeping

**SINGLE ONE**

secrets, being on the down low all of that will come back and eventually kill any relationship.

**SINGLE ONE**

## Chapter 37

### *The Last Word*
### *A Good and Perfect Father*

Last year the Lord ordered me to take a sabbatical from all ministry work. God wanted me to go into a time of rest mentally from everything. He even told me not to attend the church I Co-pastor with my husband. So, considering God's demand over my life, I

## SINGLE ONE

I decided to attend another church on Sundays until my sabbatical was over. Anyone who knows me knows just how hard this was for me. But I accomplished God's direction and was renewed in my spirit and mind.

I found myself in the church of some Pastors we are acquainted with and on this Sunday we sang the worship song, "He's a Good Father". There is a line in the song that's says, "you are perfect in all of your ways." It was during the singing of this sentence that God spoke to me.

The word-perfect means to: have all qualities and characteristics that are required to be as good as one can be. It also means to be faultless, flawless, model, ideal, exemplary, best, quintessential, unrivaled, unequal, incomparable, inimitable, unsurpassed and beyond compare. God is second to no one. He is like no other because there is no one you or I can compare Him to. God is on a level of His own making! God's thoughts are higher, and His ways are

## SINGLE ONE

better because His knowledge and wisdom are unmatched. There is

no one that can out smart Him, outwit Him, or outthink Him. He is all knowing all the time at all times. God is sovereign and He needs no one to advise Him as to how to deal with His creation. God exist outside of time and is not restricted by the time He has imposed on man for His own good. God is eternal and has always existed.

Because our God is who He is, we can trust Him to direct our lives. Our thoughts are limited by many factors, but God is not hindered by any factors. Since God has all wisdom and knowledge, He has access to our past, present, and future. Since God is all knowing He also has access to our heart's desires, thoughts, intentions, and emotions. All this information is used by God to direct our lives and to bring into our life's what He knows is good for us. Whether to build up patience for the impatient or hope for the hopeless, He knows what we need!

## SINGLE ONE

So why do we distrust God's direction in our life's? Why do we question God when He speaks to us? Why do we think we can figure out our

lives without His help? Why do we think He is unable to unravel, undo and unwind the mess we have made of our lives?

"If you believe in me and in my Father that sent me than greater things than these will you do in my name" John 17. We don't allow God to lead our lives because we simply do not trust Him to make the best choices for us! Don't sing, "He's a good Father" if you don't believe it! Don't sing, "He is perfect in all His ways" if you do not trust him to be perfect in your life!

If you do not know God as your savior consider making Him your savior today. He loves us and wants to give us love in a reciprocal relationship. God created you and loves you as His child. Why not choose Him today! If you want to welcome God into your heart today just say, "Lord I accept you into my heart. I believe in you and I need you in my life today. Wash me of all my sin and make

## *SINGLE ONE*

me your pure child today!" Welcome into the family of Christ!

## *Conclusion*

I do not profess to be an expert in marriage counseling but my husband and I have worked with married couples for about twenty years now. During that time, we became certified as lay marriage counselors and successfully wrote a marriage manual called the "Covenant Marriage Manual" that we still use today. Statistically 50% of all marriages end in divorce and among Christian Protestants that number is

## SINGLE ONE

45%. The average marriage is torn apart due to disgraceful behavioral issues. These behaviors include criticism, sarcasm, name-calling, mind reading and stone walling. Criticism is called the acid of marriage. Close behind criticism is failure to respect and communicate with each other. I wrote this book to help women and men understand each other better and to give them a good foundation as they make decisions about who to marry, why to marry and what a good marriage should look like.

Establishing a healthy marriage starts while you are still dating each other. Setting down those foundational ground rules, the non-negotiable, and the standard for respectful treatment of each other will help to promote a strong marriage. A strong marriage is the essential groundwork for building a healthy family structure that is productive and Christ centered.

A family needs involved loving caring parents and a strong relationship with God. When a marriage and a family make God the center of

**SINGLE ONE**

their family God pours out His grace, peace, joy, trust, humility, self-control and patience.

I pray that everyone who reads this book is empowered to build a great family!

www.ingramcontent.com/pod-product-compliance
Lightning Source LLC
LaVergne TN
LVHW041616070426
835507LV00008B/266